MY JOURNEY WITH ERNIE

LESSONS FROM A TURKEY DOG

HEIDI H. SPEECE

Some names and identifying information of people have been altered.

Cover Design by Michael Rehder/Rehder & Companie

Front Cover photo by Heidi H. Speece

Back Cover photo by Leigh Ann Burdett

For Mom

"Dogs have a way of finding the people who need them, filling an emptiness we don't even know we have."

— THOM JONES

CONTENTS

PROLOGUE

SPOILER ALERT: The dog doesn't die at the end of this book.

I only begin that way because like many animal lovers I can't watch movies or read books in which the dog dies. If a young lover slides into the icy depths of the Atlantic while his girlfriend hogs the escape raft, I'm fine. If a mobster is shot dead on the steps of a church while a christening is simultaneously taking place, pass the popcorn. But the minute any harm comes to an animal, I dissolve into a puddle of tears and need a few days to recover from the trauma. I've never read the ending to *Marley and Me*. I refuse to watch *Old Yeller* ever again. And as for *Where the Red Fern Grows*? Well, I think you get the picture.

So if you are like me, then rest assured that the star of this book, a mischievous golden retriever named Ernie Bert, lives a happy, spoiled, and adventurous life right to the tennis ball on the last page.

Now that I have cleared that up, allow me to explain the rationale behind this little manuscript. When I first adopted

Ernie, I knew I had a story. Not only was he from the exotic locale of Istanbul, Turkey, but during his first week in America, he committed a felony, became a social media star, and turned my life upside down. I never knew what to expect when I woke up each morning, and I still don't.

During my journey with Ernie, I've learned countless lessons along the way. Although I'm a high school teacher, he has been the true educator. It may sound cliché, but it's true. Like any relationship, he's made me re-examine a number of things in my life. Sometimes I liked what I discovered, and other times I realized that a definite shift needed to occur.

Recently, my high school seniors awarded me the honor to serve as their graduation speaker. I spent hours debating on what I wanted to tell them on their special day. To be honest, a part of me wished Ernie could talk and give the speech. That is when the idea for this little book appeared. What if Ernie could give a speech? What stories would he tell? What lessons would he teach? What did he believe to be the essential components of a happy, successful life?

If he could talk, I think he would share some of the moments I recount in these pages. I could be wrong because I haven't graduated from his course yet. However, I am delighted that you enrolled in his class along with me. Maybe you will learn something from him, or maybe it will just remind you of the wonderful power of our animal kingdom. Regardless, thank you for joining us, and now let us begin our journey with Ernie.

~Heidi

P.S. Don't forget to pack a tennis ball or two. Actually, make it three.

1

THE SADDEST DOG IN THE WORLD

On a cold, dirty sidewalk in Istanbul, Turkey, lay a six-year-old golden retriever. His expressive brown eyes followed the comings and goings of the bustling city. Buses rumbled by as residents sped to work. The call to worship could be heard in the distance. Up close, the whoosh of the air pump and the clank of a tire iron hitting the pavement added to the symphony of the streets. In the midst of it all, the dog nestled against the concrete wall, trying to stay warm as he braced himself against the blustery March wind.

This is where Ernie's story begins as we know it. What happened in his life up to this point is a mystery. Maybe he was the pampered pet of an aristocrat. Maybe he was a beloved companion to a child. Maybe he was an ignored member of a household that moved on without him. We will never know. What we do know is for several weeks the mechanics at an auto body shop threw him bits of food and let him seek shelter when the temperature dropped below freezing. At one point, a group of gypsies came by and examined him. They muttered in disgust at the ball of mange and kicked him as they walked past.

This routine continued, but the food scraps and life on the streets began to take its toll. Ernie had a bad hip, most likely because of being hit by a car, and it continued to worsen while he became thin and lethargic. As pedestrians walked past, he ignored the pain in order to roll over on his side for a belly rub or a small sign of affection. However, time was running out for the homeless dog, and he seemed to sense it.

Then on a chilly April day, a small Turkish woman known to rescue homeless dogs in the area was returning home when she noticed Ernie curled up against the wall of the mechanic shop.

"Sweet boy, sweet boy," she said softly in Turkish as she held out her hand to him. Ernie lifted his brown eyes to meet hers, and he saw something that he hadn't seen in a long time: kindness. She stroked his matted fur and gently placed a makeshift leash around his neck. With quiet encouragement, she walked him to her car.

When she motioned for him to jump inside, he hesitated and pulled back on the leash. After more gentle coaxing, he ignored the pain in his hip and leaped onto the backseat. As they drove through the city, he sat upright and watched the sights flying by the window. His panting and uneasiness seemed to dissipate. However, when they arrived at the boarding facility, he was greeted by a flurry of people, barking dogs, and something he hadn't known on the streets: wire cages.

Before they led him to one, the woman took him into a bare room with white walls and a magenta dog bed sitting in the middle of the gray floor. Ernie plodded over to the bed, sat down, and dutifully posed as a man barked orders from behind the camera.

"Otur!" he commanded, and Ernie sat. His sad eyes drooped, and his jowls hung low in a look of defeat. The white fur around his snout accentuated the pitiful look in his eyes. The camera snapped from different angles, but Ernie's expression remained the same. He had given up.

2

LOST

To understand how Ernie Bert and I found each other, you first have to meet my mother. Her button nose, expressive green eyes, pixie haircut, and petite frame are deceiving. In truth, she is a force of nature with a wicked sense of humor and a fierce determination to protect her family. As a child, my father was rarely present in my life, so Mom essentially raised me and my younger sister, Gretchen, alone. In order to stay organized and maintain a sense of order, lists became Mom's survival mechanism. She made lists of household chores to accomplish, grocery items to purchase, questions to ask the pediatrician, financial tasks to review with the accountant, thank-you notes to write, and holiday gifts to order. If something needed to be done, it went on a list.

Being the perfect rule follower, she made sure that her daughters followed suit. She never went into the express line at the grocery store if she had more items than the sign allowed, and she always took the teacher's word over ours. "Please" and "thank you" became part of our vocabulary before "ball" and "bottle," and we never went to church or the airport without bows in our hair and neatly ironed dresses.

Although Mom never pressured us to achieve top grades, she did expect us to do our best and follow a strict routine. After school, we had a snack, did our homework, ate dinner, cleared the table, watched a bit of television, and then went to bed at a set time. Rarely could we convince her to bend the rules. In fact, there is only one time I can remember when I succeeded. It was for a two-hour special episode of the David Hasselhoff show *The Knight Rider*. The fact that I remember that over thirty years later should demonstrate the rarity of such an occasion.

Mom was also the one who nurtured our love for animals. We had an army of critters that included sheep, cows, horses, dogs, cats, cockatiels, ducks, goats, and hermit crabs. With each new addition, we would argue over names like expectant parents. We had a goat named Billy, a black Labrador called Cricket, and a cat named Termite.

Mom is also the one who taught us about life and death. Whenever an animal died, she would tell us the Rainbow Bridge story. She said that our pet walked across a rainbow to a magical place in heaven where it was healthy and happy. It would wait for us until we would all meet again in heaven. After telling us this story, we had a special moment to say goodbye to our beloved animal. It was quite touching. However, on one occasion this elaborate farewell was seriously delayed.

Gretchen had a hermit crab named Sebastian after the Disney character in *The Little Mermaid*. To say that Gretchen adored this crab is an understatement. She'd sing him lullabies, talk to him as she cleaned his tank, and sit for hours just watching his every move. She'd neglect her studies to spend time with Sebastian and tell him stories.

When he had outgrown his shell as hermit crabs do, she'd go to the pet store to find a larger shell for him to grow into. This expedition could take hours until she found the perfect shell.

After he turned seven, which is incredibly old for domesticated hermit crabs, Gretchen became worried that Sebastian was sick. He wasn't moving as much, and he seemed to stay in his shell for most of the day. With final exams approaching, my sister spent her time worrying more about her crab than her grades. Mom convinced her to focus on her studies and promised to take care of Sebastian in the meantime. My sister relented and turned over the caretaking responsibilities.

One day, I arrived home before my sister, and I immediately knew something was wrong. Mom was not in the kitchen, and she was *always* in the kitchen after school. I climbed the stairs to the bedroom and found her bending over Sebastian's tank.

"What are you doing?" I asked. She whirled around with a pair of tweezers in one hand and a tube of superglue in the other.

"Sebastian is dead, so I'm gluing him back together," she said.

"What?"

"His pinchers fell off, and your sister can't know. I'm gluing him back together."

"Why?!"

"Because Gretchen is in the middle of exams. You know how she is. She'll never focus if she knows he is dead," she said. Turning to face me and to get better light from the window, she carefully placed a drop of superglue on the pincher and slowly reached into the tank for the crab carcass. With the precision of a surgeon, she squinted her eyes and placed the pincher in its proper location.

"There. We just have to wait a minute for it to dry," she said as she held the crab in place.

"Mom, that's crazy! What's going to happen when it starts to smell?"

She shrugged and said, "That's why God invented air freshener."

After the exams were over, Mom finally confessed that Sebastian had indeed gone to the Great Beyond. The tears flowed and an elaborate funeral service took place. No more hermit crabs joined the Speece family after that, though. We decided to stick with animals we couldn't reconstruct with a tube of adhesive.

As a toddler, I was a bit of an enigma to my family. I talked to my imaginary sisters named Grace and Liesl, spied on the neighbors from the top of our cherry tree, and put on plays for the birds in the backyard. While Gretchen became an avid rule follower like Mom, I was the opposite as a child. I was notorious for throwing tantrums and refusing to do as I was told, so Mom had to resort to creative parenting techniques to keep me in line.

Often during a fight, I would bite my sister on the arm. Mom told me that if I didn't stop, she would take me to a scary place called Timbuktu where bad little boys and girls went. After an epic sibling battle over a Barbie doll, Mom took me for a ride through Timbuktu. To a five-year-old, it was terrifying. It looked like a normal neighborhood, but I knew at night the monsters came out of the bushes.

I didn't completely change my ways, however, so Mom sought help from my pediatrician.

"She's a free spirit," he said, "Let her fly." So she did as best she could.

One way she did this was to encourage my love for theatrics. My dress-up bin and doll collection became my prized possessions.

That Halloween gave me the perfect opportunity to put my skills to good use. I was a ballerina, and Gretchen was a witch. We piled into the backseat of my Mom's 1980 pink Cadillac, excited to see how much candy we might gather. Unfortunately, there was just one problem. Imagine my horror when we turned the corner to find we were in Timbuktu. My eyes grew wide with fear when we arrived at the first house. Mom parked the car and handed us our plastic pumpkin containers.

"Go up and ring the doorbell," she smiled over the front seat at us. "Go on. Don't forget to say 'thank you.'" Wanting to please her, I adjusted my tutu and walked timidly to the red brick home with the large bushes in the front. Slowly, softly, I crept. Maybe if I was super quiet, the monsters wouldn't know I was there. At the top of the porch, I poked the doorbell and leaped back in fright as a loud peal rang through the house. An elderly man opened the door and offered me a piece of candy. I snatched it from his hand, spat out a quick "thankyouverymuchsir," and bolted to the end of the driveway where Mom stood watching.

I looked down at myself. I still had all of my fingers and toes, and I had a Milky Way in my trick-or-treat container. Maybe the monsters didn't know it was me! Maybe they thought I was a famous ballerina, so they didn't want to eat me! It was then that I realized the only way to be safe was to wear a costume or hide behind a facade.

That Halloween wasn't easy. But my worst Hallow's Eve came four years later at the class party, thanks again to my mother. Having outgrown the ballerina phase, I now embraced the likes of Sherlock Holmes and the Hardy Boys. I wore a brown trench coat, carried an old pipe, and sported a fedora and a construction paper mustache. Things were going great until I walked into my fifth-grade classroom after recess to find my mother standing in front of the entire class dressed as Skunk Momma — a character from a children's book about a smelly skunk that lives in a junkyard. Unbeknownst to me, Mom had signed up to be the parent host for the party. Complete with a chicken bone in her hair and blacked out teeth, she smiled a wide toothless grin and shouted, "Surprise!"

I was mortified. Our eyes locked, and I could see amusement dancing in hers. Clearly pleased that she had shocked me into silence, she chirped to my classmates and began to hand out candy. I stood motionless at the door. This put a huge damper on my cool factor. What was this little private eye to do? I could think of only one solution: act like she didn't exist. So, for the next two hours, I ignored her. As my mother prattled on and led games and sing-a-longs, I sulked at my desk and begged my friends not to talk to her. This seemed to delight her even more. The angrier I became, the more she entertained my classmates.

"Your mother is super cool!"

"I wish my mom was like that."

"Your mom is like totally rad!"

The exultations from my classmates only made the torture more unbearable. I vowed never to speak to this woman again. That lasted about a day, but the post-traumatic stress remained for decades.

IF YOU WERE to look at a family photo album, I look like the All-American little girl. Blonde hair, blue eyes, sun dresses, and freckles. I had a pony, and I played with Barbies in my spare time. I adored *Sesame Street* and *Reading Rainbow*. I loved finger painting and coloring Easter eggs. Yet, I hid a dark side.

While most children my age admired the likes of Michael Jordan and Mary Lou Retton, I had very different interests. Lucky Luciano, Al Capone, and Michael Corleone. They were my idols. Everything about the Italian Mafia fascinated me — the food, the culture, the scandal, the murder, the loyalty, the cities! It was so different from my quiet prairie lifestyle, and I so wanted to be a part of it.

I remember clearly the first time I told my mother that my goal in life was to be a mistress to a mobster. I was in elementary school, and I had no idea what a mistress was. However, I knew every mobster had one, so I figured it must be like a secretary or an accountant. I was organized and good at arithmetic; it seemed like an honorable profession and a natural choice for me. Mom was silent for several minutes and then cleared her throat.

"I see. Hmm. Hmm," she said.

To me, that was a clear signal I was on the right path, so I devoured every book and movie on the mob. Lasagna became my favorite meal, and Frank Sinatra became my musician of choice.

Why this fascination with the dark underworld of organized crime? It's simple really. I'd always wanted to be a part of a large family. Nothing made me happier than watching the Italian dinner scenes in the mob flicks. Checkered tablecloths, white twinkle lights, fettuccine, cousins fighting, mothers nagging, fathers carving the meat, grandfathers giving toasts, and the shouting. Lots of shouting. Ah, it was glorious! The added mystery and suspense that came with the lifestyle were a bonus, but the big family meals were the genuine attraction.

In real life, the nearest thing I came to having a crazy extended family was Mom's parents, affectionately known as Muckie and Bobby. During the summer, Gretchen and I would escape the dusty plains of the Midwest and fly to the lush locale of Williamsburg, Virginia, to spend time with our grandparents.

I adored life on the East Coast. Everything was exciting. We'd spend the evenings crabbing on the docks of the James River or biking on the forested paths surrounding my grandparents' home. My grandfather Bobby took us to historic sights, music concerts, and amusement parks. He was the soft-spoken, gentle, and open-minded one.

My grandmother Muckie was his polar opposite. She cursed in German, spewed advice on things she knew nothing about, and ascribed to the mantra "buck up, buttercup." While my grandfather tinkered in his workshop listening to Sousa marches and Big Band, my grandmother baked cookies to Dean Martin and yelled at the tennis and golf players on the television set. When greeting people, Bobby would offer a gentleman's handshake and politely begin a conversation about current events, political philosophy, or the latest stock prices. My grandmother's approach was much different. She quoted from the Hollywood gossip magazines and questioned the women about their manicures and hairstyles.

The one thing they agreed on was their love for animals. They had a Yorkshire terrier and a rescue cat, and my grandfather had restarted the local animal shelter that had previously closed its doors. In their garden, Muckie fed the squirrels, which ate out of her hand, and Bobby fed the birds.

Each year, my grandfather tried to increase the goldfinch population, and this involved outsmarting the resident racoon. During one face-off that will forever be a part of family lore, Bobby became frustrated that the racoon was stealing too much birdseed from his feeders. He spent hours designing and constructing an elaborate roof to prevent the four-legged bandit from reaching the seed. When this didn't work, he wired the feeder, so the racoon would receive a quick and harmless electrical jolt. This did the trick—for one day, before the animal unplugged the cord. Not to be outdone, Bobby spent the afternoon duct taping the plug to the outlet. Proud of finally outsmarting the masked varmint, my grandfather toasted himself with a martini and settled in for the evening. The next morning, he awoke to find the birdseed gone. His nemesis had chewed through the extension cord. At that point, my grandfather finally raised the white flag and declared defeat.

Each year, my grandparents' antics entertained us, and we reveled in the comedy and drama of it all. But before we knew it, our summer vacations ended, and Gretchen and I would return to Nebraska to begin the school year.

MY MOTHER firmly believed that if something had to be done, we should do it right. Having abandoned my free spirited ways as a child, I agreed. I was determined to graduate at the top of my class and go to a premier college. I studied for countless hours, peppered my transcript with extracurricular activities, and made becoming the high school valedictorian my goal.

On May 15, 1994, I gave the valedictory address at my high school; the next day I moved to Virginia to attend one of the top universities in the nation. Everything was going as planned. I was now following the rules, and it was working.

I'm not sure when it happened, but I began to mimic Mom and create "to do" lists of my own. The more lists I made, the more accolades I received. This further encouraged me to be more organized and more ambitious. After college, I got a job on live television as a weekend news reporter. It was only a matter of time before the *TODAY Show* came calling. Unfortunately, something inside of me didn't feel right. Was this really how I wanted to spend the rest of my life? Chasing a red light and pandering to a camera? My gut knew the answer—no.

That is how this straight-A student, president of every club in existence, and volunteer extraordinaire found herself struggling...big time. I had no idea what I wanted to do with my life, and that wasn't okay.

So I took a deep breath and called home.

"Hello?"

"Mom, what are you doing?"

"I'm burying St. Joseph in the yard."

"I'm sorry. What?"

"Gretchen and I are moving to Virginia to be closer to you!"

"Yes. We've talked about this. Why are you burying a saint in the front yard?"

"The house won't sell. It's been on the market for months, and I read on the internet that you should bury a statue of St. Joseph upside down to attract the right buyer."

"You're joking, right?"

"Heidi, why would I joke about this? I need to sell this house. What do you want?"

I burst into tears. "Mom, my life is a mess!" I wailed. "I don't know what to do! All of my friends have good jobs, are married, in grad school. I have nothing!"

"Oh, don't be so dramatic. Stop crying, and count your blessings."

"But nothing is going as planned!" I sobbed into the phone, searching for a bit of sympathy.

"Listen. You are only twenty-two years old. Life never goes as planned, and sometimes it turns out better. You'll figure it out. Things always have a way of working out," she said.

"I guess," I sighed, crumpling a wad of Kleenex against my cheek.

"Now, stop crying, and go read a book or something. I have a statue to bury."

So I dried my eyes and did what every rational, highly educated human being does in such a predicament. I got a job as a bingo caller on a cruise ship. I led napkin folding classes, hosted cocktail parties, and traveled to the Bahamas, Panama Canal, Scandinavia, and Tahiti.

In the spring of 2001, I learned that one of my lifelong dreams was about to come true. I was headed to Italy and the land of the mafia! Our first stop would be Rome, so I planned my visit weeks in advance by making list upon list of things to see and do. The Colosseum and the Trevi Fountain and the Vatican and the gelato stands and the Forum. Life was finally going as planned!

The number one item on my "to do" list was to find the fountain that Audrey Hepburn stuck her hand in during a famous scene in *Roman Holiday* with Gregory Peck. When the day arrived and we sailed into the port of Civitavecchia, I wore my perfect outfit. Khaki shorts and a white top. Check. I debarked the ship and caught a bus to Rome. Check. Saw the Colosseum. Check. Threw a penny in the Trevi Fountain. Check. Toured the Vatican. Check.

As the day waned, an unsettling feeling gnawed at my stomach, and I began to panic. Despite my miles of walking, I still had not found the Audrey Hepburn fountain. Where was it? It was on my list, so I *had* to see it!

In a moment of sheer desperation, I ran up to an overweight Italian woman wearing a white apron and shoved the map in her face.

"Please, help me!" I exclaimed, "I can't find the fountain! Per favore!!" She looked stunned, and then she shrugged, shaking her head in disgust.

Wiping her hands on her apron she said, "You want to see Italy? 'DIS is Italy! Look! Look! 'DIS is Italy!" Catching my breath, I followed her command. Across the street, two elderly men sat at a table drinking espresso and playing chess. Colorful scooters sailed by while elegant Italian women window-shopped at the neighborhood boutiques. Across the way, another group of men played bocce on a dusty patch of dirt in the park. Horns honked, bells pealed from the local chapel, and tourists laughed as they happily posed for pictures. Yes, 'dis was Italy, and I had almost missed it. I took a moment to look around, but again the gnawing feeling of crossing everything off my list ate away at me.

I would like to say that I stopped and chatted with the woman in the apron or joined the men for a game of bocce. I'd like to say that I grabbed a gelato and sat on a bench to soak up the Italian sun, but I didn't. I plowed forward with my face back into the map until I finally found the fountain hidden behind an iron gate. A moment of satisfaction bubbled up inside, but it quickly disappeared as I got closer to the lion's head carved into the wall. Like a good tourist, I placed my hand in the lion's mouth and pulled it out quickly, just like Audrey did in the movie. However, the magic I had created in my head leading up to the moment far outweighed the actual scenario.

Disappointed, sweaty, and tired, I trudged to the bus station in order to make the five o'clock transfer back to the ship. It was the last item on my list.

FIVE MONTHS LATER, the 9/11 terrorist attacks occurred, and the cruise line I was working for declared bankruptcy. Once again, my life disintegrated into the very chaos I tried so hard to avoid.

In a struggling economy, I grabbed hold of any job I could find. I found myself dressed like an elf at a ski resort in Virginia. Then there was the Easter Bunny impersonator in the Bahamas. The talent agent in Florida. The wedding planner in Pittsburgh. By the time I turned thirty, life was still a giant question mark. I didn't know my purpose. Then one day, I met a friend for a cup of coffee and everything changed.

It was a cold, spring day in Pittsburgh and my dear friend Josh was sick of hearing me whine incessantly about being a journalism major who now worked as a glorified receptionist for bridezillas. We decided to meet at the local Starbucks, so he could help me.

"What do you want in a job?" he asked with a steady gaze.

"Well, I want..."

"No. Write it on this napkin. Then tell me." I thought for a moment and then began to write.

"Okay," I said as I placed the pen down and slid the napkin towards Josh.

"Done?" he asked nonchalantly, as he focused on the bottom of his coffee cup in search of one last drop of foam.

"Yep. Here. I wrote 'I want a job that helps others, uses my communication skills, and incorporates my love of history.'" I peeked up at him, expecting a deep belly laugh or a serious lecture — I wasn't sure which one I would get since he was known for both.

"Duh. You should be a teacher."

"What?"

"I said, 'You should be a teacher.' That was easy." Looking pleased with himself, he proceeded to explain which schools would be best for a graduate degree in education. However, I sat in a fog. The metal chair dug into my back as the reality of the situation overcame me.

"You should be a teacher." I realized I already knew this. It is something I had known for some time. I just didn't want to admit it. Yet, now it was "obvious." I had struggled with the "what to do with my life" for ten agonizing years. Valedictorian. Summa Cum Laude Graduate. News reporter. Cruise ship hostess. Event planner. It almost seemed cruel that the answer to my angst should appear in such a prosaic manner. Even the mermaid on the Starbucks napkin seemed to laugh at me.

I wish I still had that napkin, but I left it on the table. I'm not sure who manufactures the little five-inch by five-inch paper napkins, but I owe him a thank-you and a pumpkin spice latte.

❧

I BEGAN my teaching career seven years before I adopted Ernie. After receiving my Masters degree, I secured a position teaching English at a high school in southeast Virginia. In typical fashion, I jumped into the position with every ounce of energy I could summon.

My first classroom had no windows. It was a large cream and orange cinder block room with a metal pole placed haphazardly in the middle. To make my surroundings more inviting, I went to Michaels and purchased posters with beach scenes and inspirational quotes. I worked countless hours organizing the book shelves and writing lesson plans for the opening weeks. When the first day of school arrived, I placed a piece of candy on each desk, sharpened the pencils, wrote the daily trivia and inspirational quote on the whiteboard, and plastered a welcome sign across the screen.

The administration asked every teacher to stand in the halls until the first bell rang. I did this with an exuberant smile. Pimple-faced teenagers with bed heads and sleepy eyes stumbled past, not impressed by the perky blonde who was going to teach them about the amazing world of Chinua Achebe and hyperboles. When the bell rang, I threw back my shoulders and pranced into the classroom, ready to start my new adventure. Sitting in the front row with his feet propped up on the desk was the school's 250-lb linebacker. His gigantic frame commanded the room, and the bitter look on his face told me I had met my match.

"Hello, everyone! I'm Miss Speece!" I chirped.

"And I'm Tony," he mocked as he leaned further back in his chair and crossed his arms over his chest. "You, Miss Speece, are going to hate me by the end of the year." I had just met my first student on my first day of teaching.

∽

As it turns out, Tony became one of my favorite students. He was notorious for sleeping in class, so we often gave him reading parts in which his character was comatose or bedridden. His performances were Oscar-worthy, but it was his Motown dance moves that stole the show. During our Harlem Renaissance unit, Tony took a break from his slumber to teach the class the finer points of dancing like a Temptation. As he and the rest of the class bopped to "My Girl," I realized I had finally found my home.

Tony's football sidekick Demetrius also made me and the rest of the class laugh — when *he* wasn't sleeping. One of my favorite teaching moments occurred with him during a lesson on the Founding Fathers. I asked the class which document the leaders authored in the summer of 1776. A charming but ditzy cheerleader shot her hand in the air and began waving it about.

"Ohhhhh. Myyyy. Gawwddd. I know this one! I *actually* know this!" she cried.

"Yes, Nora?"

Taking a gulp of breath, she collected herself, sat up straight, threw her shoulders back, took a dramatic pause, and proudly announced: "THE INDEPENDENCE OF DECLARATION!"

Silence. Nora looked around, expecting cheers and applause. However, her classmates and I were still trying to process her answer as we listened to the rumbling of Washington and Jefferson rolling over in their graves.

Always one with the perfect punch line, Demetrius lifted his head from his desk and said, "And there are your tax dollars at work."

∾

AROUND THE SAME time that Ernie was making his way to the boarding facility in Turkey, I found myself on the couch with my cats, Annie and Charlie, lying on either side of me. My sister, who had also become a teacher, and I were on spring break from school, so it seemed like the perfect opportunity to get my life in order. She sat on the love seat while Mom and her golden retriever Max sat on the other side, staring at me.

"Something is missing, Mom," I said with tired eyes after another sleepless night. "No matter how hard I try, I can never get ahead. I follow all the rules. I work hard. I try to do the right thing, but I'm not happy."

I knew I needed help. I had thrown my entire being into my teaching career, and it was taking a toll on my mental and physical health. I stretched myself too thin, and I became too invested in causes that I couldn't change. I wanted to be a Super Teacher and solve all of my students' problems. In the process, my social life was nonexistent, my diet consisted of sugar, wine, coffee, and carbs, and my sleeping patterns fluctuated from a few hours to none at all. The "to do" lists and countless hours of work had finally caught up to me. Like the Seven Dwarfs, I was all about work, work, work. Or, in my case, grade, grade, grade.

Charlie, my tuxedo cat, nudged my hand to pet him. I looked down into his seafoam green eyes and began to cry. Sensing my distress, Max lumbered over and lay his giant snout on my knee. He looked up at me as if to beg me to stop the tears.

"Maxxy, I love you," I said, burying my face on top of his head. Gretchen watched quietly and looked to Mom for guidance.

Mom looked from Gretchen to me to Max.

"I mean I'm forty years old, Mom. I'm single with no

family of my own. I live paycheck to paycheck, and all I do is work all day. This is not the life I planned," I cried. Max pushed his snout harder onto my leg.

Mom looked once again at Max, crossed her legs, and folded her hands in her lap.

"Well, it's really quite simple," she said. "It's time for you to get a dog."

I looked up at her, wiping my tear-stained cheeks, and I felt a combination of hope and excitement stir inside of me. A dog?

"They're wonderful companions," she continued. "Look at Max! He's always happy to see me, and when I'm having a bad day, he always cheers me up." Max returned to her side, right on cue.

"And you could travel with him and visit new places and go on walks," encouraged Gretchen.

A dog? Yes. A new companion might be just the thing I needed to bring me out of my slump and help me focus on something other than work. For the first time in a long time, something made sense. I looked down at Charlie, who had transitioned into a ball on my lap. Annie, my orange cat and the queen of the household, looked up at me with sleepy eyes to blink her approval. I mulled over the idea for a few more minutes while Mom and Gretchen continued to list the benefits of a canine companion. Looking once more at Max, I nodded my agreement.

"Well," I said smiling, "It looks like it's settled. I'm getting a dog!" Max returned to my side and once again lay his snout on my knee. "But," I added, "he has to be just like Max. Calm and obedient."

3

...AND FOUND

Six thousand miles away, Ernie batted a dirty tennis ball around a fenced lot. Throwing the ball in the air, he raced to catch it before it hit the ground. Other dogs in the yard watched as he played alone, perfectly content with his newfound toy. A green streak from an antiseptic marked the top of his head where he had an open wound.

"Dinner time!" shouted the boarding coordinator as she rattled pebbles of dry dog food in a metal bowl. The other dogs raced to their bowls, but Ernie raced to the woman's side. She sat on the ground and tried to get him to eat. Instead, he walked circles around her while wagging his tail and rubbing up against her shoulder. Cupping some of the food in her hand, she spoke soft words to him, and he grabbed a few pebbles. Then he rested his head on her shoulder and continued wagging his tail.

After a few more handfuls of food, the woman stood up and returned to her office. Ernie curled up with the tennis ball, alone once more. His eyebrows flicked back and forth as he watched the other dogs wrestle with each other. His brown eyes darkened with sadness.

In Virginia, my expression probably looked a lot like Ernie's. A few weeks had passed since my conversation with Mom and Gretchen. After much thought, I had decided that I wanted to adopt a golden retriever. Americans love the golden retriever, a breed of dog that first appeared in Scotland. A dapper gentleman by the name of Lord Tweedmouth first bred the hunting dogs in the mid-1800s, and they quickly became a status symbol for the wealthy. We know them for their golden coats, muscular builds, and gentle natures. Many golden retrievers love the water and use their swimming skills to retrieve fowl for their owners. While I didn't want a hunting companion, I loved their friendly natures and cheerful personalities. I also appreciated that they were smart, and I had never met a golden that wasn't well-behaved.

Due to my work schedule, I knew a puppy would be too much to handle, and I wanted to support an animal rescue organization. My grandfather started our local humane society, so the "adopt don't shop" mindset was ingrained in me. Years before, I had adopted a senior golden from a local organization. Buddy had been a wonderful companion, so I approached the same group once again. Unfortunately, because of a long waiting list, the director told me I would have to wait at least a year before one might become available.

Undeterred, I spent the next four weeks applying to golden retriever rescue organizations along the East Coast, only to be turned away due to long waiting lists or being outside the group's adoption radius. In the middle of my search, I found a news article about a group in Denver that rescued goldens from Turkey. Intrigued by this, I read further. Having traveled to Turkey during my time on cruise ships, I knew that stray dogs roamed the streets, but I hadn't given the idea much thought. According to the article, the canines were called Turkey Dogs. Unfortunately, dogs are not as revered or beloved in the Mediterranean and other parts of the world as they are in America. Most of the time, these canines are left to fend for themselves until a kind soul rescues them. They roam in packs on the Turkish streets or in the forests and junkyards. Once the lucky few find shelter, their rescuers fly them to America.

Sadly, the golden retriever is one of the breeds that is most often abandoned. As in America, the locals view them as status symbols, but it does not take long before their owners realize that the cute balls of fluff require a lot of hard work and patience. Discouraged by this, many people abandon their goldens, thus leaving thousands homeless and left to wander in search of food and safety. Due to their gentle natures, they cannot defend themselves like other breeds might and often perish from starvation, injury, abuse, or illness.

After reading the article I decided that I wanted a Turkey Dog. There seemed to be three relevant adoption agencies. One was in Atlanta. One was in Denver. I knew both of those were out of the question because I was too far away for them to vet me. The third one was three hours away in Washington, D.C. According to the website, a small group of volunteers ran the organization. Intrigued by this, I searched the adoption page and immediately found my dog. He was the one I was meant to have, and I knew we would be perfect together. Named after one of my favorite literary characters, Aslan was a petite, deaf golden with an angelic face. I immediately applied and waited. And waited. And waited.

Another three weeks passed, and I settled into another lonely evening on the couch. Charlie slept on the back of the couch while Annie found her spot on my lap.

With a glass of wine and soft twinkle lights on my ficus tree, I graded student essays, responded to work emails, and then I did something that I only do once a year. I cleaned out my spam folder. It seemed like a good way to take out my frustration. Click. Delete. Click. Delete. Click. Delete. Click. There it was.

In between an email that promised to increase my libido and an urgent request from my long lost, third world cousin was a message from the rescue organization in D.C. They had emailed me two weeks ago to let me know I had passed the initial screening process, and they wanted to schedule an interview. I hurriedly typed a response. This might just happen. Aslan might just be mine.

A few days passed and once again I was sitting at home alone with a glass of Cabernet, twinkle lights, and a stack of papers to grade. I turned on the TV and settled for a re-run of *Frasier*. I needed a good laugh, so this would make for suitable background noise. As I stared at the poorly worded essay that a teenager had clearly written five minutes before it was due, the phone rang with a D.C. area code. I answered, and a woman asked, "Is this Heidi?"

"Yes," I said, getting ready to tell her to stop calling and "no" I did not need a car warranty.

"'I'm with the Turkey Dog rescue." My mouth dropped open and an image of Cinderella's fairy godmother popped into my brain. The woman on the other end of the line could be the one to make my wish come true!

Allow me to pause here, dear reader. This woman did indeed become Ernie's fairy godmother, and so for the rest of the story, we will refer to her as such. However, unlike the one in the fairy tale, it took more than just a quick flick of a wand and a song to unite us. What proceeded was a series of highs and lows that stretched over three months and two airstreams before the magical moment occurred.

For the next thirty minutes, I answered questions, asked questions, and learned the story of the rescue from Fairy Godmother. Much to my dismay, she informed me that another family would soon be adopting Aslan. The family had another golden, and since Aslan was deaf, he needed a guide dog to help him navigate his new environment. My Charlie and Annie did not offer such assistance. At the end of our conversation, though, she informed me that she thought she had the perfect dog for me.

"We found a sweet boy named Eddie, and he is good with cats. He is a very good doggie."

Eddie. So, Aslan had needs that I couldn't meet, but Eddie needed a home! I looked up and noticed that my television was still playing the sitcom *Frasier*. Niles was arguing with his father while the dog sat in the middle of the couch, watching the chaos. Then it dawned on me. The dog in the show was named Eddie! It was a sign!

"Oh, he sounds wonderful, Fairy Godmother!" I exclaimed. We agreed I would send her photos of my home since I was too far away for a home inspection. If everything proceeded as planned, Eddie would be mine very soon.

I hung up the phone and immediately dialed Mom's number.

"Hello?"

"Mom! Guess what? I'm getting a Turkey Dog!"

"How?" she asked, and I recounted every moment of my conversation with Fairy Godmother.

Mom was silent for a moment, and then she said, "Well, this is wonderful news, but I need to make something clear. I will not have you calling me 'Grandma.' I want to be called something sophisticated instead."

"Goldie Hawn goes by 'Glam-ma,'" I replied.

"Mmm. No."

"Grandmother?"

"Absolutely not!" She retorted. "But...maybe Grandmummy. Like the queen."

"Grandmummy," I repeated.

"Yes, call me 'Grandmummy.' Eddie's grandmummy!" she said, clearly pleased with her new moniker.

"It's very regal, Mom," I said.

"Yes, just like me."

I SPENT the next day cleaning my house from top to bottom and taking pictures that would make any interior designer swoon. A few days later, Fairy Godmother called to tell me I passed the home inspection and all of my references gave glowing reviews. Eddie was now mine!

We scheduled his arrival for early June, which was only two weeks away. Wanting everything to be perfect for his homecoming, I made list upon list of things to buy, questions to ask the veterinarian, and tasks that I needed to complete, so I could focus on making him feel safe and loved. I purchased a new leash, collar, bed, chew toys, shampoo, and brush. I emailed all of my friends and told them to expect a baby announcement and lots of pictures in the coming weeks. I made an initial appointment with the veterinarian. Although Eddie was going to be fully vaccinated and microchipped before his departure, have a thorough exam, and arrive with his very own passport and medical file, I wanted to introduce him to the staff and doctors who would eventually take care of him in his new country.

Everything seemed in place except for one thing. I was having a hard time coming up with a middle name for my new son. I scoured baby naming websites, searched Turkish names on Google, and revisited our family tree for inspiration. Nothing seemed to work with Eddie. It also disappointed me that he wasn't appearing on the rescue's website. There were adorable Goldens of all shapes and sizes, but why wasn't Eddie on there yet? Maybe if I saw his face I would have a stroke of inspiration.

A week before Eddie's scheduled departure from Turkey, I was at Mom's, and we were planning to eat at our favorite Thai restaurant. However, this could not occur until she finished watching her afternoon news show. Never one to stray from her routine, Mom sat on the couch watching intently while my stomach grumbled for a bowl of pad Thai. I became annoyed, but looking back, I am now grateful for her devotion to schedules and the television program. Otherwise, I might have missed a call that would change my life forever.

"Hello, Heidi. This is Fairy Godmother. Ernie has had all of his shots, and he passed his medical. He will have his bath before he comes," she reported.

"Ernie?"

"Yes. Ernie."

"What about Eddie?"

"Eddie? Who is Eddie?" She asked.

"Eddie...my..." And then it hit me. I had misunderstood

his name. "Ernie! Ohhh." I tried to recover, motioning to Mom to pull up the website on her laptop and find Ernie's picture. "I thought you said his name was Eddie! His name is Ernie! Yes, Ernie!"

"Um. Okay. Ernie has had all of his shots, and he passed his medical," she repeated. Still trying to recover, I thanked her for her call and hoped that my misunderstanding hadn't nullified the adoption agreement. So what if I didn't know my son's name? Mom can't remember my name half of the time.

As Mom scrolled down the list of dogs, I anxiously looked over her shoulder. Towards the middle of the page, the saddest eyes I had ever seen on an animal stared back at me, and I saw the name underneath: "Ernie." Sitting on a magenta bed, he looked at the camera with a dejected frown on his face.

"That's him. That's my dog," I whispered.

A few moments passed as we looked at the screen. My heart ached for the sad creature that was still so far away. I wanted to hug him and assure him that everything would be okay. In that moment, I fell in love with Ernie, and I wanted nothing more than to make him smile as only a golden retriever can.

We called Gretchen and told her the news. She immediately pulled up the website on her laptop.

"Ah, Heidi. He's so sad," she said.

"I know," I said into the phone. We continued to look at his picture and the pitiful eyes staring back at us.

"He needs a middle name, Mom," I said. She thought for a moment, and then she sat up straight.

"Bert. You know Bert and Ernie. From *Sesame Street*. You could call him Ernie Bert."

"Perfect. Just like him."

4

LIKES, CAMERA, ACTION

W hen it comes to technology, I tend to move slowly. Some of my friends might say that is an understatement. I write this in 2021, and I have only had my smartphone for two years. Until recently, I relied on a flip phone and a good old-fashioned wall phone. It just seemed simpler and less chaotic.

Therefore, it should come as no surprise that until Ernie, I was a social media neophyte. I don't know how to use SnapChat. I lasted one day on Twitter, and as far as I'm concerned, TikTok is the sound of a clock. Despite my naïveté, I delved into Facebook to keep Ernie's rescuers abreast of his progress. I thought this might be a fun way for the boarding facility in Turkey and the rescue in Washington, D.C., to see the fruits of their labor.

A few days before his scheduled arrival, Charlie, Annie, and I sat on the couch, and I opened up my laptop. Charlie opened one eye to monitor the situation, while Annie lay on my keyboard as I set up the account.

Previously, I had used Facebook for about a year before I

deleted it. I found it boring, but the idea of telling Ernie's story seemed fun and rewarding.

"Do you like this picture, Annie?" I asked, pointing to one the rescue had sent me. Ernie had just had a bath, and he didn't have the forlorn look that was in his adoption photo. He didn't look thrilled with the situation, but he at least seemed upbeat. I saved it as his profile picture. Then I chose a design of the Turkish flag and the American flag side-by-side as the cover photo, and I wrote, "I'm a golden retriever from Turkey. I live in America with my family thanks to Kyra's Rescue!" I added four pictures from the boarding facility and logged off for the evening.

The next morning, I logged back in to see if anyone had joined his page. What I saw shocked me. Ernie had twenty new followers! What? I hadn't even advertised it that much to my circle of friends. I scrolled through the list of names and locations. Singapore, Canada, England, Turkey, South Africa. My Turkey Dog was becoming an international sensation!

"Mom, guess what?" I yelled into the phone. "I made a Facebook account for Ernie Bert, and he has twenty followers already! From all over the world!"

"You what?"

"I made Ernie a Facebook account, and he's famous! People from all over the world are following him!"

"I want a Facebook account."

"You wha-?"

"I want a Facebook account."

My momentary elation came crashing down as I envisioned Skunk Momma being unleashed on the worldwide web.

"Um...I'm not sure that is..."

"I want a Facebook account, Heidi. How am I going to follow my grandson if I don't have one? Come over today and make me one," she said. I knew there was no talking her out of it.

"Okay," I relented. "I'll be over later."

~

WHEN I ARRIVED at Mom's house, she opened the door, and Max greeted me. Before I could say "hello," Mom began giving orders.

"Now, I want Maxxy to be the picture that people see. Don't use my picture because there are creepers out there. I don't want someone to steal my identity. Make sure you pick a handsome picture of Max. Right, Max?"

"Yes, Mom," I said as I set up her account. "Are any of your friends on Facebook?"

"I don't know."

"Well, why do you want an account?"

"So I can follow Ernie! Don't make me friends with anyone else, though. I saw this news report where this predator logged in and..." I continued to click away and let the sound of the keyboard drone out my mother's conspiracy theories and newfound expertise on cybersecurity.

After thirty minutes and many picture vetoes later, Mom finally had a Facebook account with only one friend: Ernie. I spent the next hour trying to teach her how to navigate the website and view the updates on Ernie's account. I'll let you all imagine how that went, but it is safe to assume that I left exhausted and in desperate need of a nap and a glass of wine.

Later that night, I checked Ernie's account again. He was up to fifty followers. At this rate, I became convinced that he would break the internet. However, I couldn't get rid of the nagging feeling that I had just made a terrible mistake by giving my mother a voice on social media.

5

COMING TO AMERICA

The morning of Ernie Bert's arrival was finally here. I woke up and quickly checked my phone for an update. I had a text from Fairy Godmother. I clicked on it and scanned the contents. My heart fell, and I began to cry.

ERNIE MADE IT TO THE AIRPORT, BUT THE OFFICIALS REFUSED TO CLEAR HIM AND THE OTHER DOGS. HE HAD TO GO BACK TO THE BOARDING FACILITY. THIS HAS NEVER HAPPENED BEFORE. EVERYTHING WAS IN PLACE. I WILL CALL WITH UPDATE.

I sat on the edge of my bed, staring at the phone. I imagined him being nervous and scared as his caretakers put him in another cage and transported him to the airport, only to be returned hours later to the dusty lot and cage at the boarding facility. This couldn't be happening.

I got up and walked to the living room, where an empty bed and a stuffed elephant awaited his arrival. I knew he was being taken care of, but I desperately wanted to fly to Turkey myself to ease his fears and bring him home. He couldn't understand what was going on, and the image of those sad brown eyes staring back at me in the picture made me cry harder.

Thanks to a cranky check-in clerk and a confused customs officer, my boy's arrival was now delayed by at least a month. I was crestfallen but determined. I needed to save my dog.

Three weeks after I began my crusade to save Ernie, Fairy Godmother called to tell me she had secured a flight chaperone for him. A flight chaperone is someone who accepts responsibility for the animal and flies with it to its destination. Because of political unrest in Turkey at the time, this was harder to arrange than normal. However, Fairy Godmother prevailed, and Ernie would arrive in New York City on July 4, 2017. From there, he would travel to the outskirts of Philadelphia to spend the night with a foster family. The next day, a volunteer from the rescue would pick him up and deliver him to Washington, D.C., where I could claim him. Ernie Bert was destined to be a Yankee Doodle Dandy. From his planned arrival on Independence Day in the city where so many immigrants before him had passed, to his brief stay in the home of the Liberty Bell, to his adoption in the nation's capital, my Turkish boy already epitomized the red, white, and blue.

ON THE MORNING of July 4, I awoke with a sense of dread. What if they didn't let Ernie on the plane? I checked my messages and saw one from Fairy Godmother. He was on the flight. Exhaling a sigh of relief, I hummed a song I hadn't heard in years. I'm not sure why this tune came to mind, but it seemed appropriate. It was the theme song to *An American*

Tail, a movie that illustrates the love between two souls hoping to be reunited one day soon.

Somewhere out there, love will see us through. I willed the words to carry across the air streams and find their way to the cargo hold of an airplane with a frightened golden retriever inside. I imagined his terror as he sat in his cage and listened to the pounding of the engines. His ears had to be popping as the plane climbed higher. His heart had to be racing as luggage tumbled from the racks. With nothing but twelve long hours of travel ahead of him, my sweet boy had to be confused, scared, and lost. *Someday we'll be together, in that big somewhere out there.*

No more scraps. No more wintry nights on concrete. No more abuse from street urchins. No more fending off attacks from other dogs. No more trying to find a toy in a trash heap. The future was bright, but he just had to get to America and through customs.

Throughout the day, I tracked the flight on my computer and corresponded with Fairy Godmother. At night, I slept restlessly, but I awoke to the news that Ernie Bert had arrived safely in Pennsylvania. In just a few hours, our new life together would begin.

I quickly put on the homecoming outfit that I had carefully prepared the night before: gray pants and a red shirt to honor his home country's flag. Dangling from my ears were silver hoops I bought at a market in Kusadasi, Turkey, nearly twenty years prior. At 7am, I parked in front of Mom's house and walked up the porch steps. The front door flew open, and Mom threw her hands to the sky.

"Today, I become a grandmummy!" she exclaimed.

"You really want me to call you that?" I laughed.

"Of course! Let's go get my handsome grandson!"

We made the three-hour trek to an IKEA store just

outside of the nation's capital. The plan was to meet Michelle, a volunteer, in the parking lot. We would spend a few moments getting to know Ernie before we made the drive home.

I parked the car, and Grandmummy and I made our way to a grassy area to the side of the building. A woman with a radiant smile and golden hair held tight to a leash. The dog had his back to me as he looked longingly towards a wooded area.

"Hi, Heidi! I'm Michelle. This is Ernie!" she said. With that, Ernie turned around. Tufts of orange fur stood straight up on his head. A dopey grin spread across his face as his expressive eyes studied me.

"Hi, Ernie!" I said as I took a seat on the pavement with my legs splayed out to the sides. Ernie looked at me and then threw himself in my lap.

"He knows you, Heidi!" Michelle said as she handed me the leash. Ernie rolled on his back and licked my hand.

"Look at the love! Just look at the love!" I exclaimed. I looked up at Grandmummy as she stood over us beaming with pride.

"He's so cute!" she said. I handed her the camera, and she immediately began clicking away. Ernie continued to roll on his back with excitement as I rubbed his belly and cooed at him.

"Does he look like you pictured him?" asked Michelle. No, he didn't look the same. He looked — happy. After twenty minutes, Michelle, Grandmummy, and I agreed it was time to take him to his new home. We said our goodbyes and walked towards the car. As we neared the vehicle, I noticed Ernie was favoring his back right leg. Fairy Godmother had warned me he had a bad hip, and I knew the long flight and hours in a crate had only made things worse. I was eager to get him home to his new bed.

As we arrived at the car, I expected to have to coax him into the backseat. Surprisingly, he jumped in without hesitation and waited for Grandmummy to join him.

"Did you see that?" Grandmummy asked. "He is so smart. My grandson is so smart."

Ernie slept most of the trip with his head resting on Grandmummy's leg. Now and then, he would sit up and look over the seat to stare at me in the rearview mirror.

When we arrived at my townhouse, we discovered that Gretchen, or Auntie G as we now called her, had come over to decorate the yard and bushes with *Sesame Street* characters and "Welcome Home" signs. As we pulled into the driveway, she waved and ran to the back passenger window to look at her new nephew. As she did, she handed me a copy of the children's book *Puppy Love*. On the cover, a smiling Ernie from *Sesame Street* looks on as his new dog runs in the foreground.

"I found this and thought it was perfect," Auntie G said. As an English teacher, I had debated on which bedtime story to read to my new son. I now had the answer.

Ernie jumped out of the backseat and started sniffing his new yard. We walked around and posed for a few pictures. Then we opened the front door to his new home. He immediately transformed from a curious, playful dog to a petrified and shaking shell of himself. Cowering in the corner with his tail beneath him, Ernie refused to walk inside as his eyes flashed back and forth in terror.

"Oh, Heidi. He's scared," Grandmummy said. I bent down beside him and softly tried to reassure him.

"It's okay, sweet boy," Auntie G said, as she watched with concern in her eyes. He began to shake with fright.

"It's okay, Ernie. You're safe," I whispered, but he still refused to move. Hearing the commotion at the front door, Charlie walked down the hall to inspect. As he approached, Ernie stopped shaking and watched until the cat reached his side. Sniffing his approval, Charlie sat down as if to greet his new brother. With that, Ernie took a few careful steps inside. He looked around, and he slowly relaxed.

"Here, Ernie, look here," I whispered as I coaxed him further into the house. "Look at all the new dollies!" I pointed to the elephant and a stuffed lobster toy on his bed. Ernie took a few more steps forward and sniffed at the edge of the bed. He looked up at me, looked back at the bed, and then his entire body relaxed. The smile returned to his face, and he pounced on the elephant. Throwing it in the air, he then made his way from room to room to explore his new surroundings.

Annie jumped down from the couch and sauntered over to the new creature invading her space. She sniffed him and walked away, bored from the disruption. Charlie returned to his resting area on the back of the love seat. Yawning, he turned his back to all of us and resumed his cat nap. His job as the welcoming committee was done.

After an hour of sniffing and investigating, Ernie settled on his dog bed. With his tongue lolled to one side and a smile on his face, he let out a sigh as if to say, "Okay, I think I'm going to like it here."

That grin never left as the once saddest dog in the world curled up in a ball and fell into a deep sleep.

6

AN APPLE FOR A TEACHER

The next morning, I awoke with a start as a wave of bad breath slapped me in the face. I opened my eyes to find Ernie staring at me — the tufts of orange fur still stood straight up on his head. I had slept on the couch in order to be next to him, in case he became scared in the middle of the night. This put me at eye-level with my new companion. When I blinked at him, he broke into a grin and dashed over to grab a tennis ball from his pile of new toys. I squinted at the clock. 6:00 am.

"Ernie, it's the weekend. It's too early," I moaned, turning into my pillow. The tennis ball landed on my back — my cue to get up. I stumbled off the couch and made my way to the kitchen. Ernie bounded behind me, excited to learn our new routine. I started the coffeemaker and opened the back door to a little courtyard area. He ran out and immediately christened the holly bush. Satisfied with his accomplishment, he raced back inside and stood by his food bowl.

"You learn quickly, huh?" I said, rubbing the sleep from my eyes. I poured some of his kibbles into the bowl and watched as he inhaled them in less than thirty seconds. He turned and looked at me for more. Before I could answer, he let out a loud belch and then broke into a wide grin. He ran back into the living room and grabbed the tennis ball off the couch. Throwing it in the air, he ran circles around his bed and the coffee table while I made my breakfast.

An hour later, I grabbed the leash from its container.

"Want to go for a walk?" I asked. This would be our first official walk together, so I was nervous about how he would do. The few times he had been on the leash had gone well, but exploring a new neighborhood left me uncertain.

I held up the leash, and he looked at me puzzled.

"Walk," I repeated and bent down to fasten the leash to his collar. I led him to the front door, and he pulled back.

"It's okay," I said as he continued to pull and look behind him. "Okay, we don't have to go then." I let go of the leash, and he ran into the kitchen, picked up the tennis ball, and returned to my side.

"Do you want to take the ball on a walk?" I asked. He stood staring at the front door. I shrugged my shoulders, and off we went.

We made it halfway down the block, and Ernie watered the fire hydrant. He then turned around and made a beeline for his home. This pattern continued throughout the day. During each walk, we would get a little farther. He would leave his mark and then immediately turn around to go home.

By the end of his second day in America, I could tell that Ernie was gaining confidence, but he was still unsure of his surroundings. That evening, we finished the last lap around the block when suddenly he lurched forward and pulled me farther down the street than we had gone before. He tugged harder and harder and dragged me to where someone had dropped an apple on the ground.

I tried to pull Ernie in the opposite direction, but he refused to move. He stared at the red fruit for a moment and then gingerly picked it up in his mouth. I imagined that his life on the streets meant that he'd always dug through trash for food to stay alive. I assumed that this apple was half-eaten and rotten. As he held it and I took a closer look, I realized I was wrong. The apple he held loosely in his jaws was perfect. No marks. No worms. Just ruby red perfection.

"Why would anyone throw away a perfectly good apple?" I asked aloud. Ernie looked at me sadly as if to say, "Someone threw me away, and I was perfectly good."

When we got home, Ernie plopped the apple on his bed and fell asleep with it curled between his paws. He had found a home, and this so-called teacher had learned the first of many lessons from her Turkey Dog. Abandoned things can still be perfect and worth taking home.

BLOCK BY BLOCK, we slowly took longer walks. On the evening of the third day, I pushed it even further. When we got to where we usually turned around to head for home, I tugged on his leash to encourage him to continue. He stopped and refused to move. I took a few steps forward while he remained rigid.

"Let's go, Ernie," I said. He wouldn't budge. "Ernie, we'll just walk up the street." I took a few more steps forward. With that, he pulled backwards, stretched out his neck, and slipped his entire head out of the collar. The leash and collar dangled from my hand as we stared at each other in surprise.

Then a glint appeared in his eye as he lowered his head and bolted past me down the street. I whirled around and raced after him. People walking on the sidewalk ducked out of our way as I chased after the golden escape artist.

"Stop him! He's from Turkey!" I yelled at the confused jogger who had just dodged the furry bullet pounding towards him. Ernie reached the end of the street and turned left while I remained far behind. My lungs burned as I willed my legs to keep moving. When I rounded the corner, he was nowhere in sight. I kept running. Did he run home? No, that couldn't be! How would a dog from Turkey know where to go in America? Did he just want to go back to living on the streets? This couldn't be happening! I took a chance and headed for home. I didn't think it was possible that he knew how to get there, but I didn't know where else to search.

I reached the end of my driveway a few minutes later. There, sitting on my front stoop with an innocent look on his face and smiling from ear to ear, was Ernie Bert.

I bent over in the driveway, trying to catch my breath while Ernie barked at the front door, wanting to go inside.

"You about gave me a heart attack," I told him. Little did I know that the following day would provide another one.

7

THE FURRY FELON

Obsession is a tricky animal. In the case of Jay Gatsby, it can lead to unhealthy relationships and untimely deaths. In the case of Steve Jobs, it may give birth to revolutionary ideas and companies. As for Ernie, the effects of his obsession are still to be determined. What is Ernie's obsession, you ask? You are about to find out.

The first two days in his new home were magical for Ernie. He had fresh territory to mark — both outside and inside. He sniffed the cats, watched the squirrels, relished in gifts from friends and neighbors, and played with his toys. He especially loved the tennis ball.

If you've ever seen Tigger from *Winnie the Pooh*, that is similar to what Ernie did with his new ball. Bounce, bounce, bounce, bounce, both of them went around the house. He'd burrow it in his dog bed, pounce on it, throw it in the air, and race off to catch it again. Outside, the spectacle continued. So sweet. So innocent. So funny. That is the danger of obsession. It starts off harmless, but once it grabs hold, life for all involved quickly spirals out of control. The vortex opened on day five of our new life together when Grandmummy and I took Ernie Bert to the canine version of the North Pole: PetSmart.

"Oh, this will be such a great photo op for his Facebook fans! I'm putting you in charge of pictures when we take him," I told Grandmummy the night before. He was already up to one hundred followers, so he was averaging ten new fans a day. I envisioned him being more popular than the Kardashians and Taylor Swift. Therefore, it only seemed logical that, as a future internet star myself, I should look the part. After careful consideration, I put on a blue and teal skirt, white top, and sandals. The perfect new Mom outfit with the perfect angel-faced babe to show off in public. I was social media ready.

When we arrived, I grabbed my camera and the leash. We strutted across the parking lot and posed for a few photos along the way. Outside of the front doors, Grandmummy and I clucked over Ernie while he waited patiently to enter PetSmart. The doors slid open, and we pranced inside.

It was a scene straight out of a Hollywood movie. PetSmart employees raced up to greet us while the other customers turned to admire him. Golden retrievers have a way of attracting humans, and Ernie was no different. His newfound smile and expressive eyes made him an instant hit. Oohs and ah's mixed with "what a handsome boy" filled the air. Ernie sat regally as his adoring fans gave him treats, and Grandmummy raced around clicking more photos. My heart swelled with pride at my sweet boy and the joy he was bringing to strangers.

Then his obsession reared its ugly head. At the back of the store, there stood a massive wall of hundreds of brightly colored balls. Tennis balls. Squeak balls. Bacon-flavored balls. Ernie glanced in their direction, and his body went rigid. His eyebrows jumped up and down as he processed the motherload awaiting him. In the next instant, my shoulder was nearly ripped from its socket as a sixty-pound, drooling, orange beast dragged me towards the wall.

"ERNIE! Stop!" I yelled. My skirt flew up as my sandals skidded across the waxed floor. Employees and customers laughed and pointed at us while Grandmummy trailed behind, still clicking photos. Ernie dove under the bottom shelf of the giant display. Tail wagging and legs flailing on the concrete, he desperately tried to grab a pink tennis ball that had fallen underneath. Grandmummy arrived clutching the purse that I had dropped and trying to catch her breath.

"Oh, look! He found the ballies!" she cooed.

"Really? I hadn't noticed," I spat as I wiped the sweat off my brow and tried to gather my skirt that was showing a little too much leg. The situation before me was a dire one. The wall of balls had begun to teeter as Ernie shoved himself further underneath, trying to reach the tennis ball; only his orange tail was still sticking out from under the display.

"Oh, Heidi, he wants that ball under there. Get it for him!" Mom ordered.

"How? The whole thing is about to topple over!"

"Well, I don't know, but figure it out. He wants that ball!"

Rolling my eyes, I dutifully got on my hands and knees beside Ernie, reached my hand into a mound of dust and dog hair, and extracted...nothing. Seeing that I was attempting to help him, Ernie shimmied backward from under the display and stood next to Grandmummy to watch. I lay flat on the concrete floor and reached farther. Nothing.

"I can't get it, Ernie," I said. He and Grandmummy looked at me with a mixture of disgust and disappointment.

"For crying out loud!" I pushed myself farther. I could feel the metal case above me start to tilt again. "If this thing crushes me, and I die under a mound of tennis balls in PetSmart..." Inching myself forward, I grabbed the pink prize with my fingertips. I scooted backward, bringing dust and hairballs with me. Sitting on the ground dripping in sweat with my once photo ready hair now looking like Medusa, I presented the ball to Ernie. "Here."

Ernie sniffed it, grunted, and turned away. He looked to Grandmummy for help.

"Oh, he doesn't like it. C'mon, Ernie. Let Grandmummy find you a good one." The two of them trotted off to another display of balls, leaving me sitting on the floor. This game continued for some time as Grandmummy clucked at her "handsome grandson," and I sat back to watch. After Ernie had turned down numerous options, my patience grew thin; it was time to take back control. I grabbed a yellow one and thrust it in his face.

"Here! What about this one?" Ernie sniffed and studied it for a moment while his eyebrows danced up and down. He contemplated the option, sniffed it again, and then turned away. He walked over to another display case and studied the selection. Looking at an orange and blue ball, he gently grabbed it in his teeth and looked back at me.

"Is that the one?" I asked. He pulled on his leash to be led to the exit. He had finally found the perfect match. I looked at Grandmummy, and she nodded her approval.

When we arrived at the checkout counter, Ernie refused to let go of his new toy. I bribed him with another ball, but as soon as the staff member scanned the orange and blue ball, he grabbed it out of her hands and wagged his tail. He was finally satisfied, and we left the store mostly unscathed — until the following morning.

HAVING SURVIVED the adventure at PetSmart, we began the morning with a walk around the neighborhood. After nearly a week together, Ernie and I finally had a rhythm and a method for our walks. Quite simply, I went wherever he wanted to go. If Ernie wanted to go left, we went left. If right called to him, we went right. Only now, we had a new companion: Mr. Ballie. Ernie refused to leave the house without the orange and blue toy, so it joined us on our excursions.

It was around this time that Ernie decided that Mr. Ballie needed a friend. On this particular morning, we rounded the block and proceeded back home. With no warning, Ernie froze and sniffed the air. We were at a house on the corner, and everything seemed in order. Flower pots with impatiens and geraniums lined the walk, and a watering hose lay in the front yard. Ernie sniffed the air again and gently sat Mr. Ballie on the grass. He returned to sniffing the air. Confused, I picked up his orange ball. Ernie used this opportunity to break free from my grasp and run towards the house and a brown ball that lay hidden in the grass.

"Ernie, NO! That's not ours!" I yelled, chasing after him. He scooped the ball into his mouth and planted himself on the front porch. Whispering loudly, I urged him to drop the ball and come. He refused. He sat there with his dopey grin and a brown bulge sticking out of his mouth.

"Come. NOW. Leave it." He refused. "Ernie Bert, that

isn't yours! Stealing is bad. Come. LEAVE IT." My stern whispers weren't affecting him, so I switched strategies.

"Ernie, Mr. Ballie wants to go home, and he'll be so jealous if you bring a new ball home. You don't want to make Mr. Ballie mad, do you?" The orange bandit just sat there, smiling back at me and refusing to budge.

I panicked. What if there was a security camera or a noisy neighbor watching?

"Ernie, get off that porch NOW. Leave the ball. NOW." His grin widened.

"Oh, for crying out loud. Bring the ball and let's go."

Without hesitation, he jumped off the porch and trotted home, never once dropping his new toy until we were safely inside our house. It was official. He was now a felon, and I was his accomplice. I sat on the couch for the rest of the afternoon, waiting for the police to arrive to haul me off in handcuffs. Ernie spent the rest of the afternoon playing with Mr. Ballie and Mr. Ballie's new friend.

THE FOLLOWING DAY, I ventured out again with Mr. Ballie and Ernie. This time, I steered clear of the yards and took him to a small pond behind our development.

He trotted along, and I snapped photos to add to his social media site. As we rounded the clearing, we saw the pond up ahead. A group of ducks and a heron rested on the banks of the water.

I tightened my grip on his leash. I knew golden retrievers loved the water and game fowl. The last thing I needed was for him to drag me into the water.

The ducks quacked at us, and the heron flew to the other side of the pond. Ernie continued forward. With a flapping of their wings and a spray of water, the ducks flew to the middle of the pond and watched as we got closer. My heart quickened as I noticed the telltale signs of trouble: Ernie stopped, stood rigid, sniffed the air, and his eyebrows began to dance back and forth. He was up to something.

He took a few more steps forward with Mr. Ballie. With one more sniff, he jerked forward and jumped behind a fallen branch near the water's edge.

"No!" I shouted as the ducks flapped and quacked in fright. He pounced forward one more time, and Mr. Ballie fell out of his mouth. With his tail wagging and his snout buried in the reeds, I tried to hold on to his leash and save Mr. Ballie at the same time. Water and leaves flew up around us until Ernie reappeared with a wet and moldy tennis ball in his mouth. Pride beamed from his eyes as he brought his new prize to me to inspect.

I stood dumbfounded, holding Mr. Ballie. My golden retriever had completely ignored the ducks, completely ignored the water, and instead, he chose to hunt a tennis ball.

"Seriously? How did you find that?" I shook my head. The mallard quacked angrily. Ernie's eyes continued to twinkle as mud and pond water dribbled down his chin from the tennis ball. I praised him for his uncanny ability and giggled at how happy he was with the disgusting find. The mallard squawked another warning at us.

"Don't worry, Duckie. I don't think this retriever is the hunting dog you need to worry about," I called to him.

The four of us — Ernie, Mr. Ballie, the tennis ball, and me — returned home for a nap. We had only been together for a week, and I learned that a daily nap was now going to be a requirement if I had any hope of keeping up with my new companion.

A FEW WEEKS LATER, I decided the time had come to take Ernie to another one of my favorite spots to walk, a local nature preserve. After he had managed to wrangle free from his collar, I settled upon a harness that wrapped around his belly. It was comfortable for him, but it gave me better control during our walks. Therefore, a leisurely stroll through the woods seemed like the perfect way to spend a weekend afternoon.

We began on our normal route through the neighborhood. Ernie held Mr. Ballie as he trotted along. He had begun to do something new on our walks. When he wanted to sniff the grass, he would gently lay Mr. Ballie down and find the source of the smell. After he was done investigating, he looked up at me, down at Mr. Ballie, and back up at me. If I didn't pick up the ball and hand it to him, he would bark. This pattern continued. Stop. Drop. Smell. Bark. Being the dutiful owner, I learned to pick up Mr. Ballie and have him waiting before Ernie could become annoyed with my ineptitude.

I mention this tidbit because it took us longer than expected to get to the start of the woodland trail leading to the nature preserve. Once we reached it, Ernie seemed interested by this new location, so he and Mr. Ballie led the way down the path. Songbirds tittered from the trees, and a little brook added to the symphony. The August sun crept through the branches, but the canopy of leaves and the mossy ground covering kept us cool. I brought my camera with me, so Ernie posed for a few photos with a smile on his face and a mischievous twinkle in his eyes. This seemed to be his new trademark — gone was the sullen frown in his rescue picture.

As we rounded a corner, a flash of white caught my eye. I gripped the leash as I watched a deer jump across the path in front of us. Four more followed behind, and then they paused to study us. I held my breath, waiting for my retriever's natural instincts to take hold. He sniffed the air with Mr. Ballie in his mouth, watched the deer for several seconds, and then — nothing.

"Do you see the big doggies?" He looked at me with boredom. It now became clear that a retriever's hunting instincts had not infiltrated Ernie's DNA. He was perfectly content being the exception to the rule. Ignoring the deer, he trotted forward down the path.

Although he wasn't proving to be a retriever in the traditional sense, Ernie was a natural when it came to posing for the camera. I clicked away as he shot me backwards glances, posed in front of scenic backdrops, or lay in a pile of orange leaves with Mr. Ballie resting beside him.

After a series of photos, I had the loop of the leash around my wrist as I reviewed the pictures I had just snapped. That's a cute one. Save. Too blurry. Delete. Another cute one. Save. Blurry. Deleeeeettttteeeeee....

Before I knew what was happening, I found myself stumbling down an embankment with Ernie and Mr. Ballie racing forward. The camera bounced up and down on the strap around my neck as I desperately tried to reign in my out-of-control Turkey Dog. Brambles and limbs scratched my arms as Ernie pulled me farther off the path and into the woods.

"Stop!" I ordered. He continued plowing forward. Twenty feet from where we began, he halted. He put Mr. Ballie down and pounced on a pile of leaves. Burying the front half of his body under the leaves, he wiggled forward.

"What are you doing?" I exclaimed, still trying to pull thorns from my clothes and wipe dirt off of my face. His tail beat a rapid tattoo as he wiggled even further under the leaves. Then, like a phoenix rising from the ashes, he emerged out of the pile with a tattered baseball in his teeth. He looked at me with pride as his tail continued to flap from side to side.

"How? How did you know that was there?" I asked dumbfounded. We were standing in the middle of the woods nearly twenty feet off of the path. Yet, he had found another ball. Maybe he was a hunter, after all.

Ernie soaked in the praise that I gave him, and then he looked down at Mr. Ballie and back at me.

"What?" I asked innocently, knowing full well what he wanted me to do. He furrowed his brow and looked once again at Mr. Ballie as he continued to hold the old baseball in his mouth.

"Oh, alright. I'll carry Mr. Ballie home," I said as I picked up the orange ball. Ernie pranced forward as we made our way back to the path.

I spent the rest of our walk reflecting on the newest lesson Ernie had just taught me. To steal a line from Thoreau, Ernie marched to the beat of his own drum, and he was perfectly content doing so. As a golden retriever, his lineage suggests that he should hunt wildfowl and deer; however, my dog hunts balls. He embraces his passion, celebrates his milestones, and doesn't give a lick what anyone thinks about it. He is content in his own fur.

I admired this quality because for so long I had done the exact opposite. I followed the rules, and I caved to the idea of perfection. I wondered what would have happened if, like Ernie, I had steered off the path and not given in to the expectations of others. What would have happened if I had thrown away the map and joined the Italian men for a game of bocce? What would have happened if I had allowed myself to relax and get a few "Bs," so I could pursue other interests? What would have happened if I hadn't questioned my job switches and just enjoyed the learning process? Maybe I'd be like my golden retriever — content.

When we reached the front porch, Ernie dropped the baseball on the ground, and on cue, I handed him Mr. Ballie. He went inside and collapsed with a sigh of satisfaction on his bed. I now knew my place in this scenario, since we had practiced it many times before. I picked up the dirty baseball, washed it, and laid it beside the mound of orange fur that was once again snoring loudly and contentedly.

8

THE MVP

Since our walks began, Ernie has stolen over one hundred balls from yards, parks, picnic areas, and playgrounds. We have in our possession over twenty baseballs from the local high school, a glow-in-the-dark rubber ball, a Tennessee Vols ball from the child down the street, a neon green ball shaped like a lime, three lacrosse balls, at least thirty tennis balls from the community recreation center, and countless others that are in four large baskets throughout the house. At first, I tried to return the balls to their rightful owners; however, this only seemed to intensify Ernie's rescue missions. And most people continued to leave the balls in their yards, so Ernie ended up stealing them twice.

To make myself feel less guilty about my son's kleptomania, I've dubbed them the residents of Ernie Bert's Orphanage for Lost Ballies. Like a good soldier, Ernie will not leave a fallen ballie behind. We bring it home, clean it up, and add it to our collection.

After two months with Ernie, I found myself relaxing

with each burglary he committed. By October, I no longer felt guilty about being an accomplice, and I was understanding him better each day. Nothing, though, prepared me for what was to take place on a warm, fall night. Nothing.

GROWING up in Nebraska with familial connections in Pittsburgh, it is not surprising that football is in my blood. I grew up celebrating National Championships, AFC wins, and Super Bowl rings. When it came time for my school's homecoming football game, I convinced myself that taking him would be an ingenious idea. My students had been asking to meet him, and this seemed like the perfect opportunity to show him off.

"Are you crazy?" Mom exclaimed when I told her my plan. "He is going to run on the field and try to steal the football!"

"Don't be silly! He likes round balls. Plus, he won't be able to see the football from where we'll be standing. They'll be too many other things for him to pay attention to," I reasoned. I was right about one thing. There would be a lot of things for him to pay attention to.

That evening I dressed Ernie in a t-shirt decorated with the school's insignia, and I showed him a stuffed football toy. He sniffed it and yawned. *This is great! He has no interest in it. Okay, we can do this.* At this point in our relationship, we were still negotiating the best leash to use on our walks. I was partial to the harness because it gave me more control, but I knew Ernie preferred the typical collar. Tonight, we would go with the latter because it matched his t-shirt. Style is of the utmost importance on a public outing such as this — remember, he was a budding social media star.

As we neared the venue, Ernie's curiosity increased. The smell of hot dogs and the cheer of the crowds wafted through the parking lot. Nearing the ticket booth, I noticed my boss and a coworker talking to several students.

"Okay, buddy. It's showtime!" I said to him. Immediately, my students ran up to us.

"Oh, Ms. Speece, he's so cute! Can I pet him?" exclaimed one teenager with the school's mascot painted on her cheek.

"He's so soft!" said another as she stroked his back. Despite the adoration, Ernie continued to plod forward past his fan club. I apologized for his rudeness and shouted over my shoulder that he was eager to find the source of the hot dog smells.

As we approached the chain linked fence that lined the sporting area, I watched him carefully to see if he noticed the action on the field. He didn't. He continued past the gate, seemingly unimpressed with everything surrounding him.

Along the way, several kids stopped to pet him, but once again he ignored them. Nearing the bleachers, I noticed my friend Stacy and her husband Steve. Stacy waved to us, and I nodded as we made our way to her.

And then, it happened. Ernie stopped abruptly, stood rigid, and looked straight ahead. Thirty feet away a football soared through the air and landed in the arms of an eight-year-old boy. The freckle-faced lad yelped with glee and ran towards the imaginary end zone while his little friends followed behind.

With a powerful lunge forward, Ernie broke free from my grasp and sprinted at full speed towards the child. His muscles flexed, his legs outstretched, and his gaze steadfast.

My feet turned to cement and a cold, paralyzing sensation poured through my veins. I saw it happening, but I couldn't move. I just stood motionless as the same line repeated through my mind: "This is bad. Really bad."

Twenty feet. *Please, no.* Fifteen feet. *Please stop.* Ten feet. *Please.* Five feet. *STOP!!!* In an aerial maneuver that would rival any NFL receiver, my Turkey Dog launched himself into the air, cut the child down at the knees, and tore the ball from his grasp. The boy lay face first on the ground as Ernie jumped over him and began racing around the playground with the football in his mouth.

"Hey! That dog stole our ball! Get him!" exclaimed one of the little boys. With that, a pack of children began to chase Ernie around the playground while their parents stood watching, horrified at what had just transpired. Ernie bobbed and weaved while still holding firm to the football. A rush of adrenaline helped me regain movement in my legs, and I sprinted forward screaming, "Ernie, drop it! Drop it!"

He ignored my commands and continued to dart left and right, just out of reach of the boys and his middle-aged owner who at this point was yelling like a madwoman. All the while, a well-to-do couple looked on in utter displeasure.

"She really should have better control of her dog," scoffed the woman to her husband as we whizzed by. This continued for another excruciating minute until I managed to fling my arms around Ernie's neck and bring the game to a halt. Panting and smiling, Ernie looked at me out of the corner of his eye but refused to drop the football. I tried prying it from his vice-like grip. I tried distracting him. I tried negotiating with him.

"Do you want to go back to Turkey? So help me, I'll send you on the first flight back if you don't drop this ball," I seethed. More panting and an even bigger smile. The group of boys, their parents, my students, and several other onlookers formed a circle around me as I wrestled my golden retriever to the ground with both of us covered in slobber, dirt, and sweat. Even so, Ernie continued to hold tight to the ball.

"Give me the ball, Ernie Bert!"

Stacy and Steve jogged up to see what the commotion was about. As they neared, Stacy tried not to laugh as she took in the scene.

"Um...Heidi. Do you need some help?" asked Steve.

"I. Just. Need. To. Get. This. Ball. Out. Of. His. Mouth." I gasped. Then, while I was trying to formulate a plan, Ernie did the unthinkable. He dropped the ball. Confused, relieved, and still not convinced that his shenanigans were over, I tossed the ball to the left, and the boys raced after it. Ernie sat up and stared straight ahead. He appeared deep in thought. I narrowed my eyes and looked carefully at him. Why would he drop the ball after such a fight? He was up to something, but what?

Readers, if there is only one lesson you take away from this book, let it be this: always listen to your mother. It will save you hours of heartache when you realize she was right. It will also save you from making a complete fool of yourself as you chase after your Turkey Dog when he races towards the football field because he has just spotted the holy grail — the homecoming football.

I can't tell you the play. I can't tell you who had possession of the ball. I can't even tell you the score. I can tell you that three grown adults have never run faster than

Stacy, Steve, and I when Ernie Bert bolted from our side and bounded towards the entrance of the field.

Only this time, Ernie was outmatched; we had Steve. As both barreled towards the gate, Steve cut him off and grabbed the leash, still dragging behind him. Ernie tried to break free, but he couldn't match Steve's six-foot frame and determination to end the nightmare and get a beer.

Gasping for breath, I stumbled up to them.

"I need to get him out of here!" I took a firm hold of the leash while Steve and Stacy grabbed his rear end. Ernie refused to move. He'd already relinquished one ball; he wasn't about to let another one out of his grasp. And *this* one was the crème de la crème. No, he was going to see this mission through to the end, so he braced himself against us. I pulled. Steve and Stacy pushed. Nothing. The standoff continued.

By this time, another crowd had formed, and the spectators started shouting out advice.

"Hold a hot dog out in front of him."

"Get another ball and entice him with that."

"Have you tried reasoning with him?"

Sweat rolled into my eyes as I ignored the laughs and stares. I continued to pull and glare at him. He furrowed his brow and returned the glare. This left only one option. We would have to carry him out of the game. Since Stacy and I could not carry the sixty-pound miscreant, Steve had to do the heavy lifting. He grunted and sweated his way to the parking lot while Ernie looked over his shoulder with his tongue lolling off to one side and a satisfied smile on his face. Like any MVP that is carried off the field, Ernie seemed to be leaving with the satisfaction that he had made his mark and given it his all. The cheers of the crowd and the music from the band faded into the distance as we drove away. I looked in the rearview mirror at what I can only describe as the proudest dog in the world. He was sitting on the backseat, staring out the window with the smile of a champion across his face. It may have been his first (and last) sporting event, but I'm sure every sports commentator will agree that it was one for the ages.

9

A HUMERUS ADVENTURE

Around this time, my happy-go-lucky Turkey Dog offered a new perspective on the importance of a healthy lifestyle. During his first week in America, I had taken him to the veterinarian to have a checkup. He had all of his vaccinations, and he appeared healthy despite the limp. The vet noticed the same limp and suggested that he be x-rayed.

The technicians hoisted him onto the metal table, and he lay on his back with Mr. Ballie in his mouth. This became a photo moment and one of his first on social media. However, it was the x-ray photo that caused the most discussion.

The image showed that Ernie's right leg was not in its hip socket. It was floating with only limited support from the surrounding muscle and tendons. The veterinarian believed he had hip dysplasia, a degenerative disorder that causes arthritis. It also appeared that an accident in Turkey — most likely being hit by a car — had exacerbated it. Regardless of the cause, we had to take action quickly.

We immediately put him on a prescription diet and pain medication to alleviate any swelling. I booked an appointment with a specialist in Richmond, and we waited until they could see him. In the meantime, Ernie acted as if nothing was out of the ordinary. He continued to play fetch, chase squirrels in the backyard, and be his normal cheerful self.

When the day for the orthopedic appointment came, I loaded Ernie into the back of the car, and he, Grandmummy, and I made the trek to Richmond. The staff at the veterinary center greeted us and had me fill out the necessary paperwork. While I did, Ernie chomped and squeaked Mr. Ballie to the delight of everyone in the waiting room. I was a nervous wreck, but my Turkey Dog seemed oblivious to the gravity of his condition. To him, this was just another opportunity to be pampered by complete strangers.

Not long after, the vet technician called us into an exam room and announced that the doctor would be with us shortly. Ernie exhaled a long sigh and collapsed to the floor. The novelty of the situation had worn off, and he was ready to return home. He grunted again, looking at Grandmummy and me. The door opened, and in walked a friendly veterinarian in a white lab coat.

"Hello, this must be Ernie," he said. Ernie blinked and looked from him, to me, and back to him. Letting out another loud sigh, he rolled onto his back.

"I'm sorry, Ernie. I know this isn't your idea of fun," the vet said. Then looking at me, "I've reviewed the x-rays your primary vet sent us. I'm going to do a quick exam, and then we'll talk about options." The vet crouched on the ground to feel Ernie's joints. Ernie watched him with one eye open and appeared rather annoyed that we were disrupting his beauty sleep. After more poking and prodding, the doctor announced that Ernie had to stand up, so he could take him on a short walk.

"Get up. Up, Ernie," I said. He remained on the ground.

"He is such a brat sometimes," Grandmummy said, eyeing me with displeasure. The statement served as an obvious attack on my parenting skills. After a bit more prodding and effort, we finally coaxed him off the floor. The vet led him to a back hallway to assess his walk.

The time came for the final verdict. Ernie would need hip surgery. To better explain the procedure, the vet excused himself and returned with a set of hip and femur bones. My once lethargic dog immediately became a wolf on the prowl. One look at the femur, and a new life awakened in the golden beast.

Bark! Bark! Bark! Bark! Bark!

He jumped to all fours and let out another tirade of barks.

Bark! Bark! Bark! Bark! Bark!

When the vet wouldn't cooperate, he tried to snatch the bone out of the man's hand. Grandmummy and I tried to calm him, but to no avail. At one point, we silenced him by using Mr. Ballie as a distraction. This reprieve lasted long enough for the doctor to say, "As I was saying, we will make a small incision..."

But now Ernie saw the femur resting on the desk. He leaped towards it, and the vet grabbed it while still trying to juggle two sets of bones in his other hand. A war of wills erupted between the three humans and Ernie. He jumped on his hind legs propelled by the sight of not one but three hip bones now within his reach.

"Ernie, stop!" I scolded.

Bark! Bark! Bark! Bark! Bark!

"Here's Mr. Ballie, Ernie!" Grandmummy exclaimed, dancing around the room trying to distract him. "Yoo-hoo! Look at Mr. Ballie!"

Bark! Bark! Bark! Bark! Bark!

"Ernie, stop it! Stop it right now!" I said as he lunged at the bones in the man's hand.

"You know what? This isn't working. How about I just put these on the other side of the door?" the vet said as he frantically scooped up the rest of the skeleton and opened the door to the room. Tossing the bones in the back hallway, he slammed the door and leaned against it, ready to brace himself against the excited beast before him.

Bark! Bark! Bark! Bark! Bark!

"All gone," the vet said, displaying his empty hands. "All gone."

Ernie took a step back and stared with a pained look on his face as if someone had just served him Thanksgiving Dinner and then whisked the plates away before he could take a bite. As the electricity left the air and the vet returned to his seat, Ernie placed his forehead against the door and sighed. He let out another long exhale and melted onto the floor. For the next ten minutes, he continued to groan and sigh loudly, all the while never taking his eyes off of the door.

We attempted to ignore him, and the vet explained we could wait until the holidays for the surgery since I had to return to school in a few weeks. Based on Ernie's jumping demonstration, it was obvious to all of us he was not in pain, and the surgery could wait. I decided this was the best option since I wanted to be home to nurse him back to health.

As Grandmummy and I gathered our things, I turned to

thank the vet one more time. His back was to me, and I noticed droplets of perspiration had collected around his hairline. Sweat soaked the back of his white medical jacket.

"Thank you so much," I said again.

"Um. Yes. I'll just wait to open this door until you all leave," he said, leaning against the only barrier between the determined Turkey Dog and a pile of bones.

Ernie gave one last wistful look backwards and then pouted all the way home.

THAT EVENING, Ernie lay on the floor on his right side. His right foot rested an inch off the ground because of his disjointed hip socket. He snored loudly, and little Annie walked up and began cleaning his head. He twitched his nose, fluttered his eyes open, and then returned to snoring. Annie continued cleaning his face.

As I watched them, I reflected on the day. Despite everything — the injured hip, the poking and prodding by veterinarians, and the long car rides back and forth to exams — Ernie still could find joy in it all. Whether it was a greeting from his favorite vet technician or a fake femur inches away from his grasp, he always found something to entertain or excite. Put in similar situations, I usually stew and fret about the diagnosis, complain about the waiting time, or wish for the moment to pass as quickly as possible. I assume the worst and hope for the best. Not Ernie. He treats each moment as an opportunity.

Annie finished her cleaning session and switched to her brother Charlie, who was less than pleased. After a few hisses, she relinquished her efforts and curled up on the dog bed beside Ernie. My two orange muppets sank into unison snoring. Charlie jumped on my lap and began cleaning himself — an obvious snub to his sister. I watched the three of them and followed the lesson Ernie had taught me today. I enjoyed the moment and didn't worry about tomorrow.

10

THE LAND WHERE BALLIES GROW

F all is my favorite time of year. I love watching the changing leaves, sipping a pumpkin spiced latte, and unpacking my favorite sweaters. Maybe it is the cozy fires after a long day of work or the smell of cinnamon that seems to waft magically through the air during fall. Whatever it is, I couldn't wait to share the season with Ernie Bert.

It had been years since I had gone pumpkin picking, so I decided that would be our first adventure when the leaves began to change. I researched local pumpkin patches and found one about an hour away. It required a ferry ride across the James River, so it seemed like something fun for the entire family to do.

The night before I tried to explain the magical adventure on which we were about to embark.

"Ernie," I said as he nuzzled closer to me on the couch. "Tomorrow we are going to a special place called the Land where Ballies Grow. There are orange balls, and white balls, and green balls, and you will love it."

He snored quietly.

"Dream about the Land where Ballies Grow, and tomorrow when you wake up, we'll go," I said, kissing the top of his head.

THE NEXT MORNING, I packed a container of water, a portable dog bowl, and some waste bags for my canine companion. Gretchen couldn't join us due to a prior commitment, but Mom accepted my invitation before I could finish the sentence. So Ernie and I piled into the car and headed to Mom's. When we arrived, she walked out onto the porch and waved to us. I squinted to get a better look at her outfit. She was wearing a navy and red Navajo print pullover, jeans, and sunglasses.

"Not again," I groaned, looking down at my outfit — a navy and red Navajo print pullover, jeans, and sunglasses. For whatever reason, Mom and I have the uncanny ability to dress alike any time we go out in public. We've attended Christmas Eve service wearing black turtlenecks, black and white plaid pants, and gold necklaces. We've attended concerts sporting matching red blouses, and we've taken walking tours in khaki capris and peach t-shirts. And then there was the time that we both arrived separately in gray pants, bright green sweaters paired with a white button down top, and gold hoop earrings. Usually, we call ahead and plan our outfits to avoid the mother-daughter twinning. However, this time we had forgotten to prepare.

Shaking my head, I got out of the car.

"Oh, geez. Not again. I'll go change," Mom said, turning back to the house.

"No, we don't have time. We'll miss the ferry."

"Ernie, this is ridiculous. I'm sorry if we embarrass you

today," she said, scratching the top of his head as he leaned out the window. He looked back and forth at us, let out a sigh, and sunk into the backseat, refusing to maintain eye contact with us.

"I know, Mr. Love Monkey," I said and started the engine.

WE DROVE onto the ferry and parked near the starboard railing. I had packed a few slices of bread with Ernie's items. I rolled down the back window, and Ernie stuck his head out, breathing in the fresh air. As the ferry made its way across the river, Mom and I threw bread pieces to the seagulls that flew alongside. Ernie watched with fascination as the birds swarmed above. I captured a few photos, and Mom and I asked a stranger to take a picture of our matching outfits to show Gretchen. Twenty minutes later, the ferry docked on the other side, and we returned to the car.

The pumpkin patch was on a large farm close to Surry, Virginia. We followed a winding road past cotton and peanut fields. A few houses dotted the landscape, but miles of fields and trees mostly surrounded us.

As the road meandered past a horse pasture, Mom chattered away, and it suddenly dawned on me that neither of us had a "to do" list. Aside from finding the pumpkin patch, we both seemed content to let the day progress naturally. I smiled to myself and looked at Ernie in the rearview mirror.

"We're almost to the Land where Ballies Grow, Ernie," I said. He sat up in the backseat and panted with anticipation. A sign directed us to the entrance, and I parked alongside several others in a clearing by a giant pumpkin patch.

Children ran to and fro between a red barn and a corn maze. Families sat at picnic tables eating pumpkin ice cream or drinking apple cider. Ernie sniffed the air and his tail beat against the backseat.

"Okay, let's go," I said, opening the back door. He jumped out and looked around excitedly. His tail continued to wag as he took in the fresh sights and smells of the venue. He looked on expectantly as the young greeter handed me a map and pointed towards the pumpkin patch.

"C'mon, Ernie! Let's find you a new ball!" Grandmummy said. We walked to an area on the far south side of the field away from the other visitors. Large pumpkins peeked out from behind their vines, and smaller ones lay hidden underneath. As we strolled through the rows of pumpkins, Ernie inspected each one.

"Do you want this one?" I asked, holding out a small orange gourd. He sniffed and walked away.

"How about this one, Ernie?" Grandmummy asked, holding a larger white one. Again he walked away. This routine continued a few more times until Mom found a white one the size of a softball.

"Whaddya' think of that one, Ernie?" I pointed at the pumpkin in Mom's hand. He sniffed it and then gently took it between his teeth.

"We have a winner!" Grandmummy said, smiling. Mom and I continued to walk through the rows, searching for our pumpkins while Ernie followed behind, still holding on to his selection. After we each had settled on two medium-sized, orange ones, the three of us returned to the red barn to pay and buy a scoop of pumpkin ice cream. We found a spot at a picnic table, and I dug into the fall treat. The sweet goodness melted in my mouth as I smiled with appreciation.

"Mmm, this is so good."

"Mmhmm," Mom replied, enjoying her own spoonful of the frosty treat. Ernie gently placed his pumpkin on the ground and stared at us with longing eyes.

"Here, you want a taste?" Mom asked as she grabbed another plastic spoon and dipped it into the creamy confection to grab a tiny bite. Ernie panted and thumped his tail against the ground. I grabbed my camera to catch the moment as my Turkey Dog licked the ice cream off the spoon Mom held out for him. He smacked his lips and returned for more. We finished our portions and watched as he enjoyed the remnants from the containers.

After a few more pictures with Ernie and the three pumpkins beside a scarecrow and hay bale , we returned to the car and made our way back to the ferry. Ernie curled up on the back seat and fell asleep while cradling his white pumpkin by his side.

When we arrived home, I opened the back door of the car. Ernie jumped out with his new "toy" in his mouth and carried it inside. He immediately took it to his dog bed and fell asleep dreaming of the day's adventures. As I sat watching his paws twitch, I noticed how calm I also felt. I had forgotten how wonderful a day with no rules or lists could feel. Instead, I had a day full of memories with Mom and my Turkey Dog. I would have to do that more often, but, right now, I curled up on the couch and joined Ernie as I dreamed of the Land where Ballies Grow.

FOR A FEW DAYS, the pumpkin lay on his dog bed beside Mr. Ballie. However, by the third day, the teeth marks had worn away most of the outer covering, and it became necessary for the white pumpkin to say goodbye.

Later that week, Ernie and I drove to Mom's for a visit. When we arrived, she presented me with a gift bag.

"What is this?" I asked, looking at the bag with tissue paper poking out of the top.

"It's for my grandson. Ernie, come here," she called. He jogged over to her and sniffed the bag.

"Open it," she said, placing the bag on the floor. Ernie stuck his entire face into the bag and rummaged around until he pulled out a plastic container holding a bright red and yellow ball.

"It's a Babble Ball!" Grandmummy squealed with delight. Ernie dropped the container on the floor and looked to me for help.

"What is a Babble Ball?" I asked as I removed the toy from the plastic and cardboard.

"It's a ball that makes twenty-two animal sounds! It's going to drive you crazy!" Grandmummy said. With that, the toy let out a moo, followed by a quacking sound. Ernie grabbed it from my hand and shook it in his mouth.

"Hee-haw hee-haw hee-haw," screamed the ball now sounding more like a donkey.

"You didn't..."

"I did! Ernie needed a new ball, and this one will bring him hours of entertainment and you..." Mom laughed as the toy now croaked like a bullfrog. She reached down to pick up the tissue paper and bag off the floor.

"Do you like your Babble Ball, Ernie?" He raced after her as the sound of a screaming hyena trailed behind him.

"This isn't funny, Mom," I said, eyeing the annoying red and yellow ball that now roared like a lion.

A mischievous grin spread across her face. "Oh, I think it's hysterical!"

I spent the next hour watching my Turkey Dog play with

his new toy while I tried to figure out how to make it quietly disappear. When the ball hissed like a snake, I announced the time had come for us to depart. Mom went into the other room to grab a book she wanted me to read, so I took advantage of the opportunity. Thinking fast, I grabbed the ball and stuffed it in a drawer in the television console.

"Here you go. I liked this one," she said, returning to the room with the book in her hand. "It's a fun mystery. See what you think."

"Where is the ball?" she asked, looking around the room as Ernie pressed his nose gloomily to the drawer.

"Oh, I put it in the car with his other items while you were in the other room," I lied as I thumbed through the book. "Let's go, Ernie. Say goodbye to Grandmummy."

"Just have a quick read of the first page, to make sure you'll like it..." I sat on the front steps and a few moments later nodded my satisfaction. Grabbing Ernie's leash, we said our good-byes and got into the car.

As we pulled out of the driveway, I smiled and congratulated myself on finally outwitting my mother. Little did I know that while I was reading the first page of the mystery, she had opened the drawer, taken out the ball, and popped it into my purse. I discovered my mistake when I went over the first speed bump and a rooster let out a "cock-a-doodle-doo" from the passenger seat.

11

SKUNK MOMMA STRIKES AGAIN

Since my job requires a lot of screen time, it is nice to take a break from technology now and then. With a school holiday approaching, I announced to Ernie's growing Facebook fan club we would be "disappearing" for a week, but we would return with more pictures and stories to tell. Unfortunately, what seemed like a healthy decision on my part only served as another opportunity for Mom to wreak havoc on my life.

Sunday:

(Phone rings.)
GRETCHEN: Hi, What are you doing?
MOM: I'm just sitting down to dinner.
GRETCHEN: Oh, sorry. What's new?
MOM: I'm trying to eat dinner. Why do you always call right when I'm about to eat? Do you set an alarm or something?
GRETCHEN: Did you see Heidi is taking a break from Facebook for a week?

MOM: *(slurping a spoonful of soup)* Why?

GRETCHEN: Some social media cleanse or something.

MOM: She can't do that.

GRETCHEN: Why not?

MOM: Ernie's people need updates!

GRETCHEN: Mom, I think...

MOM: His people need him. *(Pause)* I know. I'll take over and post updates.

GRETCHEN: What?

MOM: I'll get on Facebook and post updates for him.

GRETCHEN: Mom, I don't think that's a good idea.

MOM: Why?

GRETCHEN: Don't you think she'll get mad? I mean, do you even know how to use it?

MOM: Yes. I used my first emoji yesterday! I don't care if she gets mad. He's my grandson. *(pause)* That is so selfish of Heidi not to keep his public informed.

GRETCHEN: She's going to be mad.

MOM: I don't care. My soup is getting cold. Good night.

GRETCHEN: But, Mom...

MOM: Good night.

(Click)

The next day Grandmummy opened Pandora's Box.

Monday's Post:

As Ernie's Grandmummy, I have received from Ernie's loyal public many words of "disappointment and dismay" that there are no daily updates as to what Ernie Bert is up to because his mother is taking a "vacation" from her duties as Ernie's Communications Director!.........how dare she! Ernie's "people" need to know his daily comings and goings. So on that note, I have made an executive decision to appoint myself as Ernie Bert's Press Secretary. Unbeknownst to Ernie's mother, I will do daily press briefings beginning tomorrow on his daily agenda and adventures! So all of you "Ernie fans," Ernie will be back!!!

Replies:
— *Congratulations on your appointment as Deputy Press Secretary!*
— *Never underestimate the power of a Grandmummy!*

Tuesday's Post: (in the voice of Ernie Bert)

Well, I'm baack!!!! I guess I must be like that first cup of coffee you humans must have in the morning!

My mom left a lot out about the day Grandmummy gave me my wonderful and annoying Babble Ball with 22 animal sounds...so I'll fill you in. After playing non-stop for 2hrs and 695 screeching animal sounds later, it was time to go home from Grandmummy's. Mom tried to hide the Babble Ball, but Grandmummy put it in her purse and every time the car hit a bump or she changed lanes the Babble Ball started babbling and would scream out all 22 sounds only to start all over again with the next bump!

From the back seat, I could look in the rearview mirror and see Mom's face..........her lips were scrunched up and her brow was furrowed....just like mine when I don't get my way! Let me tell you, she was one ugly, scary looking dude! I was afraid if we didn't get home soon her face was going to freeze like that!

Once home, I got Mr. Babble Ball out of Mom's purse, and we played for 6 more fun filled and noisy hours. Mom was just sitting on the couch with a dazed look on her face.........at least her brow unfurled! I think the woman is realizing that life will never be quiet or dull with ME and my balls.......I'll be back tomorrow!

Wednesday's Post: (in the voice of Ernie Bert)

Wait till I tell you what happened about 2am this morning! Annie, Mom and I were all sound asleep when Mom flew out of bed like she had been shot from a cannon to the sound of screaming!!! Mom thought one of us had been injured and was screaming in pain. But it was none other than...yep, you guessed it! It was Mr. Babble Ball's screaming peacock sound! Guess my brother Charlie was roaming the house and bumped into Mr. Babble Ball. Whoa, Mom had her scary Halloween face on, and I'm not sure, but I think she was taking Grandmummy's and Mr. Babble Ball's names in vain! Mom and Mr. Babble Ball just don't seem to be bonding, and I can't figure out why!

Thursday's Post: (in the voice of Ernie Bert)

Grandmummy and I are having sooo much fun posting my adventures on Facebook knowing my mom is CLUELESS about what we're up to! She has no idea that Grandmummy took over as my Press Secretary while she's been on her mini-vacation from her iPad. It has been so cool telling you about my daily adventures WITHOUT Mom's supervision and censoring!!! Grandmummy said when Mom ends her mini-vacation and goes to my Facebook page, she is going to turn 50 SHADES OF WHITE!!!!!!

Friday's Post: (in the voice of Ernie Bert)

Oh darn! I think Grandmummy is about to be fired as my Press Secretary!!!! We sure had fun.....Grandmummy and I sure put one over on Mom!!

Thank you Grandmummy for keeping "my people" informed

while Mom was slacking!! Grandmummy and I were a great team!!!

Replies:
— *I love Grandmummy's reporting. Could we please, please allow her to continue?*
— *Well, it looks like we need a campaign to save Grandmummy's job...*
— *Grandmummy is the best!!!!!!!*

Saturday:

Later that night, I received several Facebook notifications that I had messages awaiting in my inbox. A bit sad that my social media detox was over, I logged into Ernie's account and read my messages.

"Bring back Grandmummy! We love her!!"
"We want Grandmummy back!"
"Don't fire Grandmummy!"

"What in the world?" I thought. I went to the newsfeed and sat stunned as I read the string of posts. My mother had struck again, and now she had her own protest movement supporting her efforts. I immediately called Gretchen to find out if she knew.

GRETCHEN: *(giggling nervously)* I told her not to do it. Are you mad?
ME: I mean. How did she do it? I didn't even know she knew how to post? And she used emojis!

GRETCHEN: She is determined. Do you think someone will hack into her account? She's kind of a big deal now.
ME: They'll probably recruit her. I need to go fire her before she causes more trouble. I just...I just can't believe she figured out how to do it.
GRETCHEN: You know Mom!

LATER THAT NIGHT, I fired Mom from her self-proclaimed press secretary position. I realize that some may think I overreacted. However, they do not have over forty years of experience witnessing the inner workings of my mother's diabolical brain. I knew what she was capable of, and I knew the internet served as an addictive arsenal that she could use to create further chaos. To ensure national security and my sanity, I took the nuclear codes away from Skunk Momma.

12

TIMBUKTU REVISITED

A s I grew older, my desire to hide behind a costume only seemed to intensify, and I frequently sought jobs that required wigs and silly ensembles. At one point before I adopted Ernie, I even found myself dressed like an elf at a ski resort in Virginia.

At the resort, we had something called Teddy Bear Tuck-ins for the kids. On the days leading up to Christmas, the parents could have the resident mascot Ridgely, a large brown bear with oversized, red overalls, visit their children, read a bedtime story, and deliver a stocking full of toys from Santa. Since the staff member wearing the bear costume couldn't talk, the bedtime story became my job. I wore green tights, red shoes with bells, a Peter Pan-like frock, rosy cheeks, and a dopey hat.

On Christmas Eve, we were fully booked. We went from house to house and guest room to guest room reading "The Night Before Christmas." That afternoon a layer of ice had developed under the melting snow, so navigating the hilly terrain in felt shoes with no traction was a challenge in and of itself. This accompanied with four hours of holding crying babies, fending off attacking chihuahuas that were frightened by the giant bear, and slipping and sliding along unlit paths made for a very grumpy elf. By the end of the night, I wanted to punch Santa in his "bowl full of jelly."

At ten o'clock, we tucked in our last cherub, and I returned to my office. I had two choices. I could either change into normal clothes and delay my return home, or I could get in my vehicle dressed like an elf and be in my warm, flannel pajamas before the clock struck midnight. I opted for the latter option.

The resort was positioned at the top of the mountain with two exits. The back way was faster to my home; however, it was also narrower and had more sharp turns. There was also a slight incline to the top of the mountain to reach the crest. Having traversed the road numerous times in my trusty Bronco, I ignored the icy conditions and decided to take this route.

Happy with my decision, I turned on the radio to the holiday station and pressed my jingle-bell decked foot on the accelerator. Humming along, I made my way to the main entrance and turned right to begin the incline to the top of the mountain. I carefully navigated the first turn and then the second. A few cars were behind me, but all were keeping their distance as we cautiously made our way along the icy road. As we rounded the second bend, I saw taillights flashing up ahead. A car had slid off the road and was turned horizontally blocking both lanes.

"Oh, for crying out loud," I breathed angrily. I slowed down and came to a stop several feet away from the car. I waited patiently and prayed that the people behind me did not slide into me. They didn't, but they did slide horizontally, thus blocking the road behind me.

"Are you kidding?!" My visions of sugarplums and flannel pajamas were dashing all the way home without me. I was now stuck on the side of a mountain dressed like a Christmas elf. With a groan, I turned my tires on an angle to increase traction and put the SUV in park. I got out of the car and plodded towards the vehicle in front of me.

"Do you want me to call the police to help you get out?" I called out as I motioned to the driver to roll down his window.

"Look, honey! Santa sent an elf to help us! I told you everything would be okay!" cracked the man in the driver's seat. Clenching my jaw, I ignored him and called the mountain police.

By this time, the driver in the car behind me was able to straighten the vehicle and was now trying to navigate his way around the obnoxious driver still laughing at me. Envisioning a massive pile up that would further delay my return home, I began to direct traffic.

After several minutes and numerous honks of encouragement, the police chief and one of his officers arrived. As they made their way towards me, I continued to wave the best route for the oncoming traffic to take.

"Well, what do we have here?" called out the officer, "Did you fall out of Santa's sleigh?"

"Listen. Can you take over?" I glared at the chief.

"Busy night, huh! Tell Rudolph to watch out for hunting season! Santa is bringing me a new shotgun for Christmas!"

"Chief, she already knew that! She works at the North Pole!" His sidekick guffawed. The two doubled over with laughter as I attempted to march angrily back to my vehicle. However, I ended up sliding most of the way there, so the bells on my hat and toe shoes sent off jingles into the night sky that were only masked by the peals of laughter from Barney Fife and his sidekick.

Once in the car and halfway down the mountain, I began to relax. I could still make it home before midnight and forget the nightmare of the previous five hours. Tomorrow, I'd be at Mom's eating ham and scalloped potatoes. We'd open the gifts first while Gretchen took lots of pictures...PICTURES! Arg! I forgot that I had to have the pictures from the Teddy Bear Tuck-ins developed by December 26 in time for the departing guests to collect them. There was no way I was going to go to Walmart on Christmas Day, so it was now or never. I had to get them developed.

Groaning and dreading the trek to the box store, I turned up the volume on the holiday classics. *This will be okay. It will be fine. No one will be in Walmart at eleven o'clock on Christmas Eve.*

Thirty minutes later, I pulled into the barren parking lot; I knew my theory was correct. No one would see me. I could make this a fast and uneventful trip.

By this time, my feet were frozen, and the green tights I wore could no longer block the frigid winter wind. I grabbed my purse and ran towards the door. They opened, and I quickly made my way to the film drop off. Past the kitchen utensils and dish towels. Past the toilet bowl plungers and bath rugs. Past the oversized stuffed animals and furry pillows. Past the bikes and helmets. Finally, the film slot. I stopped, caught my breath, and opened up my purse. Aside from my wallet, it was empty. I had left the disposable camera in the car.

At that moment every painful memory of the evening replayed in my head. The itchy tights. The crying babies.

The blinding flashbulbs. The attack dogs. The slippery sidewalks. The rude jokes. The frigid temperatures. The stupid drivers. The laughing police officers. Everything bubbled up and like a volcano I spewed out a chain of expletives.

"&^*!*&@! %$^&!%%$#$@#!^#*%#^%!%!" I seethed.

I exhaled. *Ahhhh...that felt good.* With a newfound calmness, I turned around only to be met by an image that remains imbedded in my mind forever. There standing before me was a Norman Rockwell family — a mother and father decked in their Sunday best stood holding the hands of two towheaded toddlers dressed in velvet and patent leather shoes. An angelic light glowed about them as they stared at me in horror.

I was standing in Walmart on Christmas Eve dressed as an elf, and I had just cursed like a sailor in front of the all-American family on their way to midnight mass.

"Mommy, that elf just said a bad word," said the little girl on the verge of tears.

"No, honey," the mother whispered as she quickly pulled her children away from the scene. "That's not an elf. That's just a crazy person. Let's go say a prayer for her."

ONE WOULD THINK that after that incident and my childhood trauma in Timbuktu I would have outgrown my love of dress up. Unfortunately, I hadn't.

With Ernie's first Halloween fast approaching, I searched online for the perfect costume for us. Beauty and the Beast? No. Thing 1 and Thing 2? No. Dorothy and the lion? No. After several days, I got frustrated. My lunch breaks became consumed with Amazon searches, and my afternoons were filled with trips down the aisles of Michaels and PetSmart looking for inspiration. Nothing seemed just right for such a momentous occasion. The clock ticked down, and Halloween was only a few days away. I had to decide.

During a game of fetch in our backyard, it finally came to me. I knew exactly what I wanted us to be, but it required some creation on my part. I returned to Michaels and purchased white puff paint and a neon yellow t-shirt. I used the paint to draw two curved lines on the front of the shirt. Setting it aside, I opened up my iPad and placed an order on Amazon. In twenty-four hours, our costumes would be complete. As I did this, Ernie watched me out of the corner of his eye. He knew I was up to something, and he wasn't sure whether to give his approval.

"Just you wait," I told him. I knew he would love it. The next day, my package arrived, and I opened it up in my bedroom. It was just what I wanted, but there was a part of it I had to hide from him until the big reveal.

Grabbing the t-shirt, Amazon package, and a pillow, I called for Ernie, and we headed to Grandmummy's house. When we arrived, I quickly put the t-shirt on, stuffed the pillow underneath, and tucked the shirt into my white jeans. Turning to Ernie, I took a black bellhop hat out of the package, careful not to reveal the item sewed on top. Slightly amused, Ernie jumped out of the car and walked up to the front door, wearing the hat. We rang the bell and waited.

Grandmummy opened the door. It took a moment for her to register the scene before her, and then she began to laugh. I had transformed into a giant tennis ball, and Ernie was wearing a black hat embroidered with "Fetch Champion." On top of the hat was a yellow tennis ball. He was completely oblivious that such a prize sat perched on his head. However, he seemed to embody the essence of his role.

"I love it! Let's show the neighbors!" Grandmummy said. Enthused by the attention, Ernie marched proudly through the neighborhood as Grandmummy introduced him to her friends.

"Look at my grandson," she said proudly. I waddled along behind, trying to keep the pillow from sagging and making me look like a middle-aged woman with droopy implants and an absurd passion for neon yellow. After our Halloween parade ended, I finally showed Ernie what he had perched on top of his head the entire time. He clamped down on it and smiled his golden grin. It was then that I realized the joke was on me. He had been patient with me for dressing him up, but what he really enjoyed was being himself—the Fetch Champion of the world.

That's the thing about Ernie Bert: he is confident with whom he is. He has a limp, chipped teeth, cowlicks, and bad breath. If that isn't good enough for someone, so be it. It doesn't bother him. He doesn't need a new outfit, a spa day at the groomers, or an abundance of likes on social media. He just wants Mr. Ballie and a full belly. The critics can step aside because Ernie Bert is only going to be one thing: Ernie Bert.

After our Halloween escapade, I began to capture his self-confidence and his lopsided grin on camera without the silly gimmicks. Where I used to make him pose with wigs or stylized backdrops, I now tried to capture authentic moments we shared together. One of those snapshots won a small prize from the Virginia Veterinary Medical Association. It will never win a Pulitzer, and it certainly doesn't belong in the National Portrait Gallery. However, it is a testament to the magic that can happen when one throws away the costumes, takes off the stage makeup, and embraces oneself. It requires much less energy, and it is much more pleasant than green tights or traveling to Timbuktu in a tutu.

13

THE TEACHER'S PET

Despite spending several months with Ernie, I still hadn't relaxed my obsessive need to prove myself at work. My employer recognized my work ethic, so he continued to add more responsibilities to my already full agenda. Still desperate to please, I ran myself ragged. I'd grade papers at four in the morning. I'd answer parent emails over the weekend. I'd offer homework advice to students late at night. It took Ernie and his mischief to finally knock some sense into me, and it happened during a weekend visit to school.

I woke up on a Saturday morning, and I felt an immediate sense of panic when I realized I had left a set of essays on my desk at school. As I drank my morning coffee and watched Annie give Ernie his daily forehead cleaning, I devised a plan. No one would be at school at this hour, so I could take Ernie with me. He could explore the building while I made photocopies and collected the essays.

"Hey, Big Guy." His ears perked up, and he rolled his eyes to look in my direction. Annie placed her paw on his snout to keep him still while she finished her grooming.

"Want to go to work?" I asked. He jumped up and broke into his lopsided, golden grin. Annie scolded him and walked off, angry that she hadn't finished her job.

"C'mon. Let's go."

The parking lot was empty when we arrived. Ernie's tail thumped on the back seat as he seemed to recognize the location of his MVP status just a few months before at the football game. I secured his leash and collar, and he jumped out of the car. Zig zagging his way to smell every blade of grass, he led me to the back door.

After we entered, Ernie passed several lockers and then stopped in front of one. Sniffing up and down the metal door, he took a step back and barked. After teaching for a decade, I should have predicted this moment. Teenagers leave and forget all sorts of food items in their lockers. The mold and fungal populations in these metal containers would leave even the most legendary botanist amazed. Apparently, Ernie had discovered a thriving colony that met his satisfaction.

"Leave it," I commanded. I pulled out a few kibbles of dog food from my pocket and diverted his attention away from Locker 109.

We made our way to my classroom, and I closed the door behind us. Letting Ernie off the leash, I logged in to my computer and began to organize the files on my desk. Ernie sniffed the room for a few minutes and then stopped in front of the bookcase. He stood at attention and growled.

"Quiet," I mumbled as I reviewed the first essay.

"Why can't these kids capitalize proper names?" I thought as I angrily scribbled in a red pen. Ernie growled again. I continued to ignore him.

Halfway through the essay that was now covered in red ink, I felt a nudge on my side. I looked down to see Ernie sitting proudly before me with a glass snow globe in his mouth. Several years ago, one of my students went to London and returned with the gift. It always had a special place on my bookshelf, but now it sat precariously between a set of canine teeth.

"Ernie, no," I said, "That's not a ball!" Before I could grab it out of his mouth, he dropped it on the concrete floor. Miraculously, it didn't break. Ernie ran a few steps back and waited for me to throw his new "toy" across the room. I cradled the glass globe in my hand and placed it high upon the bookshelf. This infuriated Ernie, and he began barking.

"C'mon, let's go to the library," I said, grabbing my files and quickly logging off the computer. I put his leash back on as he continued to bark and growl at the "toy" that remained out of his reach.

"Ernie! I want to show you someplace fun!" I said, tugging on his leash. He finally gave in and followed me out of the room. As we made our way to the library, he stopped to sniff every piece of furniture along the way. When we entered the library, I did a quick scan of the room. No balls. No round objects. Just books and the copy machine.

"I think we're safe," I thought as I once again let him off his leash. I had brought Mr. Ballie to keep him occupied, so I threw it to the other side of the room towards the biography section. He raced after it and returned it to me. He jogged a few steps back like a linebacker waiting for a pass from a quarterback. I threw it again, and this time it landed in the children's section. He bounded after it, and I turned to the copy machine. I once again became immersed in the job at hand, and I failed to keep a close eye on the furry mischief maker.

After the last copy, I turned around, but Ernie was nowhere to be found.

"Ernie?" I called. Silence. "Ernie! Where are you?" I dashed towards the children's nook. He wasn't there. I looked in the computer lab. Nothing.

"Ernie Bert. Where are you?" I heard a jostling by the librarian's desk and ran over to it. There sat Ernie, happily gnawing on the librarian's stress ball she had left on her desk.

"Ernie! You are going to get me fired!" I scolded as I gathered up the foam pieces that littered the floor, and I tried to hide them under a pile of papers in the trash can. It was time to return home. This was clearly not one of my better ideas.

I collected my belongings and dragged my dismayed golden retriever to the back door. As we made our way past the glass case displaying the student artwork, Ernie stopped and braced himself against my forward motion.

"What?" I said exasperated. I looked in his direction at a colorful display of clay bowls.

"Good grief, Ernie," I spat. "Those aren't balls either! Let's go!" I jerked his leash as he continued to look back at the pottery treasure. As we neared the exit, Ernie gave one final sniff towards Locker 109.

On the drive home, I looked in the rearview mirror. He stared back at me with a pleased look on his face. I thought more about our visit, and I laughed at the ridiculousness of it all. Ernie had thwarted every attempt I had made at doing work on a Saturday morning. Instead of grading papers or checking emails, I spent the morning chasing after my dog and his insatiable love for anything round. I had to admit that, despite the brief moments of panic and impatience, it was a lot more fun than the way I had planned to spend my day.

By the time we got home, I had come to the conclusion

that I would not grade the essays that sat on the passenger seat. Instead, I would play fetch with Ernie and take him on another adventure. And that is exactly what we did.

After a weekend of playtime, a visit with Grandmummy and Gretchen, and a tour of the historic streets of Colonial Williamsburg, we settled in for a relaxing Sunday evening by the fireplace. For the first time in a long time, I felt refreshed and ready to tackle the challenges of the school week ahead. The essays remained untouched in my car, and I now had a weekend full of memories with my dog and family.

As I sipped my tea, I smiled to myself, wondering what my boss would say if he only knew the chaos my Turkey Dog had caused at school.

ON MONDAY MORNING, I awoke with newfound energy, and I practically skipped into work. My boss greeted me at the front door in his customary formal manner. He nodded towards me.

"Good morning, Heidi," he said as I returned his greeting and nod. "Oh, Heidi..."

"Yes?" I asked as I turned to look at him.

"Ernie left his ball in the library. It's at the front desk." He looked me up and down and turned back to greet the students entering behind me. I whirled around. There sitting in all its glory at the welcome desk was Mr. Ballie.

"That little rascal," I said under my breath. I couldn't help but laugh as I snatched up the ball. I had just been caught breaking the rules, and it felt — good.

14

A SKELETON IN THE CLOSET

As the months passed, Ernie Bert gained weight on his frail frame. He strengthened his muscles with countless games of fetch, and his coat came in shiny and thick thanks to his nutritious diet. The time for his hip surgery had finally arrived.

I couldn't sleep the night before because I knew the pain Ernie would be in after the procedure. I tossed and turned. At one point, I got up to stroke his head as he slept restfully. Unimaginable scenarios ran through my head. I tried to remain positive, but I kept returning to the worst-case scenarios. What if this was the wrong decision? What if he had a complication during surgery? What if this made his hip worse? What if...

"Wait a minute," I thought. "Remember the lesson Ernie taught you after the last vet visit. I wasted my time worrying for nothing." I repeated this over and over to myself, and I decided to force myself to approach the following day in the same happy-go-lucky manner as my dog. Worrying hadn't served me before, and I doubted it would do any good this time either.

THAT MORNING we played one last game of fetch, and then we made the drive back up to Richmond. The technician called us into the exam room, but this time there weren't any skeletons.

"I learned my lesson," joked the vet as we entered the room. He looked at Ernie, who had once again dropped to his side bored by the entire situation.

"Let's go for a walk, Big Guy," he said, and Ernie hopped up, eager to leave the drab surroundings and find the missing bones.

"I'm going to take him back and do another exam before we get started."

The minutes ticked by. I waited and waited and waited. Then I panicked. What was wrong? Why was it taking so long?

"Stop worrying, Heidi," I told myself. I focused on the pictures in the room and the landscape scenes transitioning on the desktop computer. My heart stopped racing, and I could feel my body becoming less tense. After twenty minutes, the door opened and in strolled Ernie Bert with his lopsided smile.

"Hi, buddy! Were you a good boy? Were you?" I asked, reaching down to pet him.

"He was, and...I don't think he needs the surgery."

"What?" I asked.

"I don't think he needs it. I actually had another specialist look at him, and he agrees. It seems his body has grown scar tissue around the area to support the bone. At this point, we would consider the surgery a success if he was walking at eighty percent what he is doing now without the surgery," the doctor reported.

I broke into a wide grin. Was I hearing this correctly? Ernie didn't need the operation?

"Really?!"

"Yes, he is getting around well and seems to have adapted to his injury on his own," said the doctor. "It just goes to show you what a healthy lifestyle and love can do!"

I walked out of the vet clinic, somewhat dazed at the news, while Ernie strolled along. He stopped briefly to look back at the door, knowing that a pile of bones still lay out of reach. Then we both exited the building happy, grateful, and worry-free.

15

THE VALEDICTORIAN AND THE DROPOUT

O nce I knew Ernie wasn't in pain from walking and sitting, I enrolled him in obedience school. Since I had a history of academic excellence, I assumed my son would follow suit. We weren't going to win the Westminster Dog Show, but we could certainly graduate summa cum laude from sit, stay, heel. This would be our chance to show the world a perfect partnership of intellectual prowess.

We met in a large church parking lot surrounded by trees. There were to be seven other dogs in the group. A corgi, that was already well-trained, greeted us while a Bernese Mountain dog and a Vizsla stood by a clump of trees. Several mutts joined the group a few moments before class began. However, it was a German Shepherd puppy that caught my eye. Her young human seemed laid back and friendly, but I could see the look of competition in the dog's eyes.

The shepherd's owner, another couple, and I were exchanging small talk when Grandmummy arrived. She waved me over to her car, so I excused myself from the conversation.

"Look what I got Ernie for his first day of school!" she exclaimed, pulling out a miniature backpack with his *Sesame Street* namesakes sticking out from the top. "His own little backpack!"

I laughed and placed the backpack on Ernie. He posed for a few pictures for his Facebook fans, and then he trotted over to join the others.

"You know, Heidi. I think he could be the valedictorian," she said, eyeing the competition.

"Yeah, sure," I said as we walked towards him. The other owners had formed a small group and some of the dogs played with each other while others sat nervously off to the side.

"Actually, maybe he *could* be the valedictorian," I thought as I continued to size up the rest of the group. With that, the instructor called us to the middle of the parking lot, and Ernie's first day of school began.

At first, Ernie loved everything about obedience school. He enjoyed meeting the other dogs, and the tummy rubs seemed endless. The best part for him was the large plastic container holding the dog treats. He didn't get to enjoy those at home since I tried to avoid overly processed foods or treats, so this was a new and exciting experience. I tore up one of the jerky bits into pieces and fed them to him one by one. When the group finished with introductions, the instructor called for the class to begin.

With the first command, the German Shepherd snapped to attention and effortlessly demonstrated the sit position. My gut told me she would be our chief adversary on our road to winning the top spot. At this point, you are probably wondering why a woman in her forties with a graduate degree would lower herself to an intense competition with a dog. It's simple. I'm a competitor at heart. If I see someone doing something, I am determined to do it as well or if not better. I expected my son to be the same. I expected him to want to win as much as I did. I expected him to care as much about trivial competitions as me.

Unfortunately for me, Ernie could have cared less. Instead, he was refusing to leave the jerky container and join us in the parking lot. The instructor told me I needed to be firm and in control. What she didn't understand is that no matter how hard I tried, Ernie would remain defiant until he got his way. After more loud barks from him and "firm" commands from me, we came to a compromise. I put a few jerky bits in my pocket, and he joined the rest of the class.

This spectacle did not go unnoticed. Not only did I have to contend with the watchful eye of the dog that I now dubbed "Miss Goody Two Shoes," but I had to endure a critique session from Grandmummy after each class. Each night, she brought a lawn chair and camped out on the sidelines watching us train. She analyzed the other dogs and gave us her coaching notes on the drive home.

"You know, Heidi, that German Shepherd didn't sit properly on the second command. I think if you work with Ernie this weekend, he has a shot at overtaking her."

"Mom, this isn't a competition," I responded, even though I was in full warrior mode.

"Oh, I know. But you just need to work with him. He'll get it."

The rational side of me told me to enjoy the time with my dog and focus on him, but the high school overachiever and consummate perfectionist in me spoke louder. After that first evening, I became determined that my dog would end up at the top of his class. It was time to make a list and a training schedule.

The next day after school, I placed a few kibbles of his food in my pocket, and we went for our afternoon walk. He ambled along on our normal route when I startled him by stopping suddenly.

"Ernie, sit!" He looked at me confused. "Ernie, sit." He tilted his head to the side.

"Ernie, sit." He tilted his head to the other side. "Sit. Sit."

He slowly lowered his back end to the ground.

"Good. Stay. Ernie, stay," I held up my hand to motion him to stop. He tilted his head again.

"Stay. Stay." I took a few steps back.

"Good boy. Come!" I held out a handful of kibbles, but he remained firmly planted on the ground, still confused by this sudden change of routine.

"Ernie, come!" Realizing that the strange episode had ended, he jogged forward and grabbed the food from my hand. I repeated this five more times on our walk. At first, he seemed hesitant and confused. By the fifth time, he appeared annoyed, but he followed my commands on cue to placate me.

I repeated our mini-lessons each day during our afternoon walks. By the following week, I felt confident for our second class. This time when we got there, we found a cheering section. Under a tree to shade them from the sun sat Mom and her two bosses, Denise and Roger. Grandmummy worked part-time at a window furnishings store, and Denise and Roger were avid golden retriever fans. They once had a golden of their own, and they smothered every dog they came across with attention. Ernie was no different. In fact, the two had dubbed themselves his honorary godparents. Seeing the three of them sitting expectantly in their lawn chairs at first amused me. But then, the butterflies began. Would Ernie execute everything we had practiced this past week, or would his cheering section be disappointed? We were about to find out.

The instructor called us into the middle of the parking lot, and I glanced over at the German Shepherd who was sitting at attention. Ernie was sitting, too; however, he had his back to the instructor and remained focused on the treat container on the other side of the parking lot. The instructor reviewed the agenda for the evening, and Ernie continued to stare at the jerky treats sitting twenty feet away.

When it came time to demonstrate the skills we had been practicing, Ernie decided to perform since he had an audience. He sat on command and did not flinch a muscle during the stay portion. After twenty minutes and fully expecting a treat for his Herculean effort, he pranced over to the jerky container. This time he waited politely for a treat. I was amazed. Could this be a turning point for us? Was I now in charge, and had he become my pliable student?

"Go, Ernie! Go!" cheered Grandmummy, waving at us. Denise clapped her hands while Roger sat with a proud grin on his face. I smiled back, nervous but hopeful.

Once the five-minute break was over, the rest of the owners and their dogs dutifully walked up to the instructor and stood patiently. After some tugging, Ernie slowly followed me halfway to the group. Then with a sigh, he slumped to the ground and lay on his side, exhausted by the idea of learning another command and entertaining his entourage. I tried to bribe him with treats, compliments, and encouragement. Nothing worked. Ernie was done.

"Heidi, it looks like Ernie has reached his limit. You can take him to the sidewalk and watch the rest of the lesson if you like," offered the instructor. I walked sheepishly towards his cheering squad.

"Well, that didn't go so well," Grandmummy said, studying her grandson.

"It's okay, Ernie! You're tired, aren't you, my handsome boy?" said Denise. Roger continued to smile and offered a hardy belly rub when Ernie lay down in front of him. Ernie had given all he wanted to give, and we could expect nothing more from him. We sat and watched the rest of the group practice the "come" command — Ernie still lying on his side watching out of the corner of his eye and me sitting on the pavement beside him wondering where I went wrong as a mother. Why hadn't my love for learning translated to my son? Was I destined to have an obedience school dropout? This could not be happening.

"That German Shepherd is really good," said Grandmummy.

"Oh, I know," said Denise. "And so pretty, but not as pretty as my handsome boy!"

I am ashamed to admit it, but I became jealous. Why couldn't my dog finish the lesson? Why couldn't he be the star of the evening — especially when "his people" were present? The night ended on a somber note as we said goodbye to Grandmummy's bosses, who must have been less than impressed. Ernie, on the other hand, found renewed life when I announced it was time to go home. He sprang up and ran towards the car.

Despite the step backward, I became even more determined that my dog would learn the commands and be ready for the next lesson. I refused to accept that "Miss Goody Two Shoes" would win the coveted top spot without a fight.

Each day after school, I grabbed his leash, and we

practiced sit, stay, and come on our walk. While I waited for my dinner to cook, I'd call him into the kitchen.

"Ernie, sit. Stay. Come. Good boy!" Soon he anticipated my commands and would sit before I could utter a word. I gave him extra kibbles for this and breathed a sigh of relief and satisfaction.

The following Thursday, we arrived ready for school. Once again, there sat Grandmummy in her lawn chair. This time she was joined by her neighbor who had an unruly dog herself. I felt better about her being there to watch than I did Grandmummy's bosses. At least she would understand the insurmountable odds I faced.

The lesson proceeded as usual: a few treats to begin, review of last week's commands, a brief introduction of a new command, some practice time, and a break. Things went well, and Ernie and I received praise from the instructor on our progress. I beamed with pride while Grandmummy and the neighbor gave us thumbs up from the sidelines. Smiling to myself as we trotted over to the plastic container, I felt a renewed confidence and determination. We were back on track! There was just one problem; Ernie was on a different track. This became apparent when the break ended, and the instructor called us to the center of the parking lot.

Once again, Ernie refused to get up. This time I grabbed a large treat and held it in front of his nose. Intrigued, he slowly stood and followed me to the center of the parking lot with the other students. Success! I listened carefully as the instructor showed the "down" command with the German Shepherd. All the other dogs and students watched with rapt attention. Six wet noses and pairs of dark brown eyes stared at the grace and ease with which Miss Goody Two Shoes performed the command on the first attempt. A twinge of jealousy tore through me again as I watched the four-legged teacher's pet. *Oh, Heidi. Stop! Ernie is doing just fine.* I looked down at him to give him a reassuring smile. Unfortunately, his focus was not on the lesson before him. Instead, he had turned his back to the instructor once again and was staring at the treat container. I lightly tugged his leash to regain his attention. He looked up in boredom and sighed. I tugged again and whispered, "Ernie, turn around and pay attention. The shepherd is outshining you."

Ernie let out a loud belch and turned around in slow motion. Once he had repositioned himself to face the teacher and his peers, he let out an annoyed groan and collapsed to the ground.

"Is Ernie done for tonight?" laughed the teacher. I looked at Miss Goody Two Shoes who watched with a tilt of her head. Her owner giggled at my mound of fur now sprawled on the ground.

"Oh, no! No no no... He's not! C'mon, Ernie. Up! Up!" I responded. I refused to let the perfect canine and her owner outperform us tonight. This meant war.

"Ernie, get UP," I ordered through clenched teeth and smiling lips. Nothing. "NOW." Nothing. Grandmummy watched in horror from the sidelines. Time stood still as I contemplated my next move. Do I yank the leash? Prod with baby talk? Use the final weapon in my arsenal — the jerky stick? I opted for the latter. Slowly pulling the treat out of my pocket, I locked eyes with my golden retriever.

"If you get up and finish the lesson, you will get this jerky stick," I told him. Eyes locked. We were at a standoff. It became a battle of wills, but I still held the jerky stick. After several intense seconds of glaring at each other, Ernie slowly and deliberately rose to his haunches and sat at my side. I gave him a portion of the treat, and the class applauded.

"Yea, Ernie!" cried Grandmummy, beaming with joy. I looked at the German Shepherd and smirked.

"Mmm hmm... look who is about to steal your thunder now, missy!" I thought. My smugness lasted one night. The rest of the lessons proceeded as such: treat, lesson, practice, break, refusal to sit up, frantic negotiations, defeat. It eventually became the joke of the class that if Ernie was going to learn anything, we had to cram the lesson into the first twenty minutes. Everyone else seemed amused by this but me. My son was going to be the valedictorian whether he wanted to be or not. Yes, I had turned into one of *those* parents.

On the second to last night of the course, the instructor gave us a handout with all the commands Ernie had to master before he would earn his diploma. The final exam would be the following Thursday, which left us only seven days to review eleven weeks of material. Once again, I came home each night and worked with him in the backyard or on our walks. We intermingled the lesson with some fetch time as a reward. Ernie seemed to thoroughly enjoy this, and he progressed rapidly through most of the commands. The only one that stumped him was "down."

"Ernie, down," I said, pointing to the floor. He blinked back at me. "Down. Ernie, down." Nothing. After several days of no success, it finally dawned on me why he wouldn't follow the command. It was his hip. Although he could walk and sit with ease, the movement to the down position was causing him pain, so he simply refused to do it. We needed to find a compromise.

"Ernie, look. Down. Down," I said as I gently pushed him onto his side. "Good boy. What a good boy! You don't

have to go down on all fours. See. This works! Good boy!"
He wagged his tail as I gave his belly a rub and continued to
compliment him.

Once I showed him he could lie down on his side rather
than on all fours, he performed the task on cue. We were
ready for the final exam.

Thursday came, and I awoke with an unsettling feeling. I
had to go to work, but all I could focus on was the
countdown to the final exam.

"Ernie has to do this. He has to get a diploma," I moaned
to my colleagues. "If he doesn't, I will be a teacher with a
dropout for a child!"

When the day finally came to an end, I rushed home.
We still had enough time to get in one more review session
before we had to leave. Sit. Stay. Down. Up. Come. Heel. No
matter what command I gave him, Ernie executed it
flawlessly.

"This is going to happen," I told him as I took a deep
breath. It was time to leave. He hopped into the backseat,
excited for a new adventure. It didn't take long for him to
realize that this was the same "adventure" that we had gone
on for the last eleven weeks. Disgusted by the banality of it
all, he laid down and fell sound asleep.

When we arrived, Auntie G, several neighbors, and
Mom were sitting in their lawn chairs, ready to cheer from
the sidelines. Mom had a disposable camera to snap
pictures while Gretchen had a bouquet of flowers on
her lap.

"Yeah, Ernie! You's can do it!" yelled one neighbor in a
thick New York accent. My anxiety level crept higher. I
looked back at Ernie, who was staring at me with sleepy
eyes.

"Okay, big guy, let's do this!" I chirped, trying to sound

confident and elated by the upcoming task. Now the butterflies had turned into vultures attacking my stomach. I got out of the car and opened the back door. Ernie jumped down and let out a loud belch.

"BUUUUUURRRRRPPPPP!!!!"

"Excuse you!" I scolded him as his peers looked my way in disgust. "It was Ernie. Sorry! So sorry!" Miss Goody Two Shoes batted her brown eyes at us and then looked up sweetly at her human. *See, Daddy, he's not refined. I told you he was just a street dog.* For one last time, Ernie and I made our way to the circle of dogs and humans in the parking lot.

"Ernie Bert is here," announced the instructor, "That means we have to hurry and get everything done in twenty minutes before he quits on us." The others giggled and agreed. I smiled meekly and tried to laugh it off. I looked at the German Shepherd, and her eyes met mine.

"It's on," I thought.

Ernie sailed through the sit, stay, and come commands. The next one would be the down command. If he could get through this, I knew we were home free. We walked around the parking lot. All eyes were on us. Grandmummy watched with her hands clenched in her lap, for she too knew the gravity of this moment. As we neared the instructor, I stopped. Ernie stopped at my side and sat. I told him to stay, and he did.

"All you have to do is lie on your side, Ernie. That's it," I whispered to him. Taking ten paces forward, I turned around and faced him. He sat there obediently and watched me. His body remained rigid with anticipation.

"Down!" I commanded, pointing to the ground. He stared back at me. I drew in a quick breath. "Down!" He stared back at me. "Please, pretty please. Down?"

Then he leaned forward on his two front paws and

slowly maneuvered his way to the ground. He didn't resort to lying on his side to protect his hip like we had practiced. Instead, he seemed to realize how important this moment was to me, so he lowered himself to all fours. Once he reached the ground in the classic down position, he looked up at me, broke into his golden grin, and began panting.

At that moment, I didn't care if we graduated from the course or finished the rest of the commands. My Turkey Dog was trying to please me, even at the expense of his own well-being.

"Oh, Ernie, come, come!" I cried to him. He gingerly rose to his feet and then trotted over to me. I buried my face in his neck.

"I am so sorry, buddy. I am so sorry. Thank you for doing that, but I will never make you do that again. Do you hear me? Never." I looked into his dark brown eyes.

"That was great, Heidi. Are you ready to finish?" called the instructor.

"Um, yes. I wasn't expecting him to do that because he has a bad hip. That was...that was really amazing," I said, looking down at my loyal companion. "C'mon, Ernie, let's go finish this, so we can go home."

The last few commands went just as planned, and the instructor happily declared that we had passed the course. Once we received the news, Ernie plopped to the ground and rolled on his side. He was done. He had lasted twenty-five minutes. A record.

I sat on the cement with him and watched the other dogs make their way through the commands. The German Shepherd finished with ease. The beagle plodded along angrily. The lab still pirouetted through most of the maneuvers, but even he passed the course. At the end, we gathered once again in the middle of the parking lot for the distribution of diplomas.

When his name was called, Ernie didn't budge. I took a few steps forward and pulled on his leash. Nothing.

"Here, Ernie! Your diploma!" called the teacher. Nothing.

"Ernie! You worked so hard! Go get your diploma!" Grandmummy called from the sidelines. Still nothing.

"Go, Ernie, go!" cheered another neighbor. With that, he slowly rose to his feet and followed me to the center of the circle. We posed for a quick photo and returned to the sidelines, where he once again dropped to the ground. After the ceremony, we returned to our cheering squad who gave me the bouquet of flowers and Ernie a new ball. This was followed by more pictures, more congratulations, and more barking at the jerky treats. As we made our way to the car, I noticed the German Shepherd and her human to my right. We walked over to them.

"Your dog did such a great job," I said to the young owner.

"Thank you so much! She is still a puppy, so I wasn't sure how it would go," he beamed. "I think we might do the advanced class!"

"She would be great at that. I think Ernie and I are going to skip it," I said, looking at Ernie. He licked my hand in agreement. My Turkey Dog had competed every day on the streets for a scrap of food, a warm place to sleep, and a handout from a stranger. He was tired of competition because it no longer meant life and death. It meant silly pieces of paper to hang on a wall or a plastic statue to gather dust on a bookshelf.

"This was such a great learning experience for the dogs," the man said.

"Yes, it was," I replied. "And for the humans, too."

～

WHEN WE RETURNED HOME, Ernie collapsed into a deep sleep on his bed with Mr. Ballie. I put the flowers Mom and Gretchen had given me in a vase, and I placed Ernie's backpack and diploma on the bookshelf. I sat on the couch and logged into Facebook so I could report the successful end to our evening. The computer pinged as a notification announced a new post on his page.

Ernie, Grandmummy is so proud of you! You made your mom look so good at obedience school! YOU showed her how to do all the commands. Look out Harvard! Here comes Ernie Bert!

I smiled at Mom's excitement and the fact that she had once again taken over his Facebook account. I looked over at my exhausted companion, who snored loudly. Ernie's diploma doesn't say "valedictorian" or "summa cum laude" on it. In fact, every dog who took the class ended up passing, whether they knew the commands or not. That's okay. There are much more important things in life than perfectionism and accolades. Ernie taught me this. I may not have a Harvard-bound canine, but I have Ernie Bert, the Fetch Champion and my loyal companion. That is more than enough for me.

16

NAUGHTY OR NICE

Holiday traditions have always been an important part of our family's Swiss heritage. Every Christmas, my grandmother made moon cookies, baklava, and springerles. As we decorated the tree, my sister and I would hide a pickle ornament and later write letters to Santa. These traditions made the holidays extra special, and I wanted to continue them to some degree in my home. During our first Christmas together, I discovered the perfect opportunity for Ernie Bert and I to create a new tradition.

In a mindless fog on my way to work, I noticed an advertisement outside the local garden center. "Get Your Pet's Photo with Santa this Saturday" it declared. Perfect! Ernie could pose with Santa Claus, and we would send the photo out as a Christmas card for all to enjoy.

At the end of the day, I raced home to announce my plan to Ernie Bert. He greeted me at the door, tail wagging and tongue hanging out, excited by my arrival.

"Guess what, Mr. Love Monkey? You're going to get your photo taken with Santa Claus!" I said. He hopped up and down and ran circles around the living room like a greyhound at a racetrack.

"Yes!" I squealed, urging him on.

"Bark! Bark! Bark!" he yelped with excitement. He stopped mid-circle and slid the rest of the way on his hind feet until he stopped at my side. Flopping himself over on his back, he wiggled his feet in the air as I patted his spotted belly and laughed at his delight.

After a quick walk and snack, we nestled onto the couch and scoured websites for a holiday sweater. I no longer felt the need to find costumes for Ernie, but a Christmas sweater was different. This separated a civilized Turkey Dog from a street urchin. The challenge soon became which one to choose.

"How about this one?" I asked, pointing to a blue and white striped sweater with a giant penguin on the back. Ernie refused to look at me and remained focused on Mr. Ballie. "Too childish?"

As I scrolled through the pages and pages of options, I became more confused. Would he look okay in red, or would it clash with his reddish orange fur? If I go with the tartan plaid as a nod to his Scottish roots, should I choose the red and white option to honor his Turkish heritage? Or, do I opt for the giant Christmas tree embroidered on a white background to make a statement? Then again, there was the faux Burberry design that would look dashing on him.

"Ernie, which one?"

A red and white striped sweater with a reindeer embroidered on the back appeared on the screen. He sniffed the screen and belched loudly. I took that as a "yes," so I hit "confirm order."

A few weeks later, the photo day arrived. I wasn't sure if I could be in the photo or not, so I spent countless hours surveying my closet and debating on whether to make a quick trip to the mall. I settled on a festive red blouse, a new pair of jeans, and my black leather boots. Ernie donned his new sweater, jumped into the back of the car seemingly pleased with himself, and off we went to meet Santa Claus.

When we arrived at the greenhouse, I parked and went inside to survey the setup. A decorated garden shed stood behind the main building, and a staff member sitting at a table surrounded by ferns and poinsettias directed me there. Inside, Christmas music and jolly laughs from Santa Claus filtered through the air. A cheerful couple greeted me and pointed to the right side of the shed with a large chair and staging area. A young girl and her terrier waited in line with her parents. Santa sat perched on a bench with a white curtain, twinkle lights, and scarlet and gold bulbs hanging from the ceiling. A photographer clicked pictures and gave directions to the family posing with their lab mix.

"This is so fun!" I said. I ran back to the car, and Ernie Bert jumped out without hesitation. I adjusted his sweater and patted down his fur that always managed to stand straight up between his ears. When we entered the main building, I steered us to the left to a walkway leading to the back of the store and a holiday shed. Halfway down the pathway, Ernie stopped. I continued to move forward and tripped backwards as he tugged on his leash.

"This way! You have to get your picture with Santa," I said. He continued to tug. Turning around, I saw the reason for his distraction. Above us, and displayed in a soft, warm light, sat hundreds of Christmas balls made of glass. He let out a deep, continuous growl. His eyebrows jumped back and forth across his forehead, and his tail began to wag.

Bark! Bark! Bark!

He struggled against the leash as he wiggled and jumped with excitement from tree to tree.

Bark! Bark! Bark! Bark! Bark!

"Ernie, those aren't balls! They're decorations! Here! Look!" I grabbed one of the glass globes and let him sniff it. He lunged forward and tried to grab it with his teeth.

"No!" I cried as I imagined glass shards shattering in his mouth. This only caused him to bark even more and begin what he thought was a game of fetch. By this time, everyone in the store stood motionless as the dog in the reindeer sweater careened back and forth through the displays. He jumped over a basket of garden gnomes and raced to the other side of the store, hoping I would throw the decoration. Knocking over a metal snowman, he skidded to a stop, barely missing a display shelf filled with holiday trinkets.

Bark! Bark! Bark!

"Ernie, come here! Those aren't ballies!" I turned to the shop owner. "I am so sorry! He is addicted to balls, so anything that is round he assumes is a ball."

She offered a thin smile and pointed to the shed. "The photos are back there."

"Yes, yes. I'll get him there. I am sorry. I'm so sorry. He thinks they are balls!" As I continued to apologize and beg for forgiveness, an elderly sales clerk with pink cheeks and a warm smile made her way towards me. In her hand, she held a tennis ball.

"Here. See if this helps," she offered.

"Thank you so much! I meant to bring his ball in case this happened, but I forgot," I sputtered. "He's really a good dog. He's from Turkey, and he just loves ballies, and we're starting a new tradition to see Santa, and I didn't even think to bring his ballies because he just loves them. He's obsessed with balls, and Ernie, stop!" I snatched the ball from her outstretched hand and rushed to collect my dog, who was now eyeing a basket of felt snowballs.

"He's just adorable," chuckled the elderly woman.

"Mmm hmm," said the store owner through pursed lips.

I waved the tennis ball to grab Ernie's attention, but he ignored me while he chewed on the snowball. I grabbed his collar and tugged firmly, causing him to spit out a slobbery, felt wad on the floor.

"Leave it," I ordered and jerked the leash, dragging him to the shed while holding the tennis ball like a carrot. It worked, and we made it to the check-in table. Now sweating profusely, I rubbed my elbow against my forehead and managed to smear makeup all over my sleeve. Ernie's reindeer sweater had twisted to the side, and the orange wisps of fur on his head stood straight up like a character from *The Little Rascals*.

The couple that I had met moments before during my initial canvassing greeted me again. The husband nodded while on his cell phone, and the woman directed me to sign in while she explained the process. The photographer would take two photos, and then I could decide which one I wanted to keep. The entire process would take twenty minutes, since only a few people were in front of me. My breathing started to return to normal, and I straightened Ernie's sweater. Licking the inside of my hand, I tried to flatten the cowlick at the center of his head. My efforts didn't work, but I knew his imperfections were part of his charm.

"Cute dog," the little girl in front of us said as she patted Ernie. He had calmed down and now sat studying the man in the red suit and white beard who was trying to get a terrier to look at the camera. Ernie licked the little girl's hand and then rolled down to the ground to lie on his side while we waited.

"What a sweet boy," the girl's mother said, nodding her approval. I smiled as my confidence returned.

"I think we can do this," I thought to myself as I let out a long exhale.

A few minutes passed, and the sweat evaporated from my brow. Ernie continued to lie at my side quietly. His eyebrows jumped from side to side, but he seemed relaxed and tired from his previous antics. Suddenly, an energetic beagle came bounding into the room, pulling a young man who gripped the leash with both hands. A woman pushing a stroller and grasping the hand of a little boy struggled to keep up. The man did his best to control the beagle, but the dog had other plans. Ernie remained relaxed and began gnawing on his new tennis ball, seemingly oblivious to the loud entrance of his canine counterpart.

The man mumbled a quick apology and looked back at his wife and children who had joined him. Having just enjoyed ten calm moments with my own bundle of fur, I smiled smugly at the man and watched as he continued to struggle with his anxious dog.

"Okay, the pizza is on its way," the elderly man on the cell phone said to his wife as she nodded and collected money from the beagle's owner. The dog had his snout in a basket of pet toys and began emptying them one by one onto the floor. Meanwhile, Ernie remained at my feet, gnawing on his tennis ball.

"I wish our dog was as good as yours," the woman nodded towards Ernie as she balanced a baby on her hip and clutched the hand of the little boy who now sat in the stroller.

"Thank you," I smiled demurely. "He is a good boy. Aren't you, Ernie?" Ernie cocked his head up a few inches and arched an eyebrow while continuing to work the ball along his molars.

"Our dog needs some training," the husband said, putting the wallet in his back pocket while keeping a firm grip on the beagle that was now sniffing Ernie's unmentionables.

Proudly, I told them about Ernie's valedictorian status in obedience school and passed along the name of his teacher. I'm not sure how it happened, but in a matter of ten minutes I had turned from a parenting nightmare into "Mother of the Year." All the old competitiveness and perfectionism which I thought I had overcome came roaring back. And Santa was now only steps away.

The photographer motioned us forward. When I tugged on Ernie's leash, he jumped to attention and carried his ball to Santa, sat obediently beside him, and flashed his golden smile for the camera.

"Your dog is a pro!" the photographer and Santa declared in unison.

"I know. He's on Facebook," I boasted. "He's used to having his picture taken."

"He certainly is. What a handsome dog!" the photographer said looking at the images on the camera, "To be honest, both shots are great."

"Oh, we aren't picky," I replied, noticing that I had suddenly inherited a Southern drawl. "Either one'll do."

"It will take about fifteen minutes to print, so if you just want to wait back there, that would be great," the photographer gestured. "Bye, Ernie Bert!"

"Say, buh-bye," I responded with my new accent. I smiled at the envious beagle family and paraded my Kennel Club Champion to the back of the shed. He looked at me for his new tennis ball, and once again lay on his side, gnawing the ball in his teeth. After about twenty minutes of sitting, my right leg bounced with boredom. I sighed and stood up. In the queue, the beagle was drooling over the crying toddler in the stroller.

"Bless their hearts," I said smugly to myself.

I had to get a breath of fresh air. Wrapping Ernie's lead around the leg of the chair, I moved to the open doorway and breathed in the crisp December air. Winter had arrived in Virginia. As I gazed out at the white lights sparkling in the trees, memories of my grandfather came to mind. Every Christmas Eve, he recruited Gretchen and I to help him make luminarias in the driveway leading up to the house. He told us that the residents of Bethlehem created the same effect when Jesus was born to lead visitors to the stable. As children, Gretchen and I would follow my grandfather with a wheelbarrow full of sand. We'd fill each of the brown paper sacks with sand and a votive candle. We'd then place the paper sacks an equal distance apart. Our measurements had to be precise, and only at sunset could we light the candles. As the sky grew darker, the anticipation grew. Any moment, my grandfather would give the signal to light the candles and...

"That dog just stole our pizza!" yelled the woman at the check-in desk.

My mind struggled to return to reality as an orange blur came racing past me with a giant piece of pepperoni pizza in his mouth.

"Ernieeeeee!!!!" I yelled as my adrenaline kicked into action. An elf jumped out of the way of the incoming retriever with mozzarella dripping from his teeth. Weaving in and out of Christmas trees and poinsettias, I tried desperately to gain some yardage on the Turkish thief. As the chase ensued, Santa roared with laughter and the customers in line howled in delight at the spectacle. Nearing the exit, Ernie lowered his head and extended his body to its full potential. I saw my chance. I grabbed the end of the leash that was flying through the air. However, Ernie's momentum caught me off balance, and instead of gaining control, we both plowed through the line of patrons, barely missing the beagle family.

In that brief but everlasting moment, the beagle's mother caught my eye, and I noticed a smug smile on her face. As Ernie continued to drag me forward with tomato sauce and pepperoni leaving a trail behind us, I knew exactly what she was thinking: "Bless their hearts."

17

THE BEST WORST DOG EVER

E verything changed on the day that Grandmummy broke her wrist. And not just any wrist — her dominant one. To most, this may seem like a minor hurdle. Most times, this would be true. However, in this case, there was another factor to consider: Limerick.

Let's rewind a bit.

SETTING: August 2018. A quiet Virginia town.

CHARACTERS: A lonely woman who had recently lost her beloved Max. *(This is Mom.)* Two opinionated daughters. *(Gretchen and me)*

(Phone rings.)
ME: Hello?

FAIRY GODMOTHER: Hello, Heidi! It is Fairy Godmother! I found the perfect doggie for your mom! His name is Limerick.

ME: What is he like?

FAIRY GODMOTHER: So sweet. So calm. Loves cats. Perfect for your mom.

ME: Great. When do we pick him up?

FAIRY GODMOTHER: Tomorrow.

ME: See you then.

This isn't how the actual chain of events transpired, but it is Mom's version. It is also how Limerick, the "sweet, calm, perfect doggie" entered our lives and quickly turned them topsy-turvy with his shenanigans.

Like Ernie, Limerick came from Istanbul, Turkey. The same woman who found Ernie outside of an auto body shop discovered Limerick roaming the streets. While Ernie had a pitiful look of hopelessness in his photos, Limerick had a big grin and a happy-go-lucky twinkle in his eye. He was whiter than Ernie and had a big black nose and floppy ears that stuck out resembling the likes of Dumbo or Yoda. My sister and I determined that this sweet, calm dog would indeed be the perfect companion to cheer up our mother who had lost her beloved Max a few months prior. So, on a balmy September afternoon, Mom and I made the long drive to the nation's capital to claim the newest member of our family.

Limmy was everything that Fairy Godmother claimed he would be — until we got him home. With a sniff of the air, he smelled the cat and tore through the house in search of his new roommate. Thankfully, the calico fur ball showed her claws, and Limmy's hunting instincts were extinguished after a quick swat at his nose.

Never one to be discouraged, Limerick pranced over to the brand-new loveseat, lifted his back leg high in the air, and christened his new home. Gretchen raced to find a rag and soap, and I stood there amazed at the spectacle. Did I just see that correctly? Our Turkish contortionist had lifted his back leg perpendicular to the floor, pointing his toes directly at the ceiling while simultaneously sending a horizontal stream of urine to the back of the couch. He repeated this athletic feat several more times over the coming weeks, and each time his form improved. His leg lifted straighter, the toes pointed tighter, and the stream of urine shot out farther.

WHILE I APPRECIATED the athletic artistry of our new family member, Mom remained wary. She had been used to calm and obedient Max. Limerick proved to be the exact opposite. It took some time for the two to reach a compromise, and, at first, I received nightly phone calls with crisis updates from Gretchen.

(Phone rings.)
GRETCHEN: What are you doing?
ME: Eating dinner.
GRETCHEN: Oh, sorry. I think Mom is going to have a nervous breakdown.
ME: Why?
GRETCHEN: Limmy christened both couches again. He keeps barking at the geese, and he nearly took down the china cabinet.

ME: He's a dog. That's what dogs are supposed to do.

GRETCHEN: Heidi, I think she is going to lose it.

ME: She already has.

GRETCHEN: That's not funny.

ME: She'll be fine. I want to go back to my dinner.

GRETCHEN: Did you see we might get a hurricane next week? I was watching the news, and they said we should...

ME: Gretchen, we are not getting a hurricane. I want to finish my dinner.

GRETCHEN: Well, you should stock up on toilet paper, batteries, water. Oh, and do you have an emergency radio? You might...

ME: You need to be like Ernie and me. Don't worry. Be happy. Goodbye.

(Click)

AFTER A FEW WEEKS, the frantic updates subsided, and Mom did not have the nervous breakdown as predicted. Instead, Limmy and Mom had settled into a new rhythm. He seemed to calm down as the excitement of his new surroundings wore off, and Mom found humor in some of his antics.

They also began to bond over their daily training session. Mom did not enroll Limerick in obedience classes. Thanks to Ernie, we had learned our lesson. That said, Mom decided there was one command that she wanted him to master: smile. Yes, smile. Why this took precedence over sit and stay, I could not tell you.

Regardless, Limmy and Grandmummy worked diligently, and after a month, Limerick learned how to smile on command. He would sit, point his face up, spread his upper gums, and squish his snout into the most ridiculous grin one can imagine. His crooked teeth and squinting eyes added to the slightly terrifying spectacle. Mom squealed with delight each time he did this. I was less than impressed.

AS THE HOLIDAYS APPROACHED, Mom purchased little gifts for the neighbors and friends in the area. Many of them enjoyed gardening and bird watching, so she found presents to encourage these pastimes. One of these gifts was an edible bell made of millet, sunflower seeds, peanut butter, and dried blueberries. According to the salesclerk, many songbirds such as cardinals, finches, Jenny wrens, and chickadees would flock to the bell. Unfortunately, she forgot to mention that Turkey Dogs named Limerick might also be partial to the tasty treat.

Without thinking, Mom put the bell, still wrapped in its shopping bag, on the center of the dining room table, along with several other purchases. Out the door we went to do more shopping. When we returned, Limerick greeted us with a giant smile. However, this time, he looked like Jed Clampett from *The Beverly Hillbillies*. Sunflower seeds and millet created a toothless grin that would rival any backwoods moonshine maker. Limerick's tail bounced up and down as sunflower seeds spurted from his mouth.

"Nooooooooo!!!! Oh no!! Limerick!" yelled Grandmummy, as she lunged for the half-eaten bell. He wrinkled his nose even more and squinted his eyes. Holding up the gift that now dripped bird seed and dog slobber, she ran to the phone to call the vet.

"It has blueberries, peanut butter, sunflower seeds... yes... um... millet... this can't be happening... mmhmm... I have no idea! It was in the center of the table, and nothing else appears to be disturbed....mmmmmhmmmm....oh, geez....I mean this dog....okay....you're sure?....okay....I'll watch him....okay....thank you so much," she panted as she hung up the phone with a wild look in her eyes.

"What did the vet say?" I asked as Limmy continued to smile while I tried to remove pieces of seed and millet from in between his teeth.

"She said that nothing in the bell will harm him, but he will probably have an upset stomach. I'm to monitor him. This dog..." she said as she collapsed on the love seat and put her face in her hands. Limmy walked over to her and once again broke into his signature smile.

"It will be okay, Mom. Look at him. He's fine!" And he was. For the next three days, whenever Limerick went for a walk, he left a trail of birdseed droppings behind him. I started calling him Tweety and giggled at the image of my mother, her Turkey Dog, and a flock of birds following behind.

"Mom, you should sing, 'Feed the Birds' when you take Tweety for a walk!" I laughed.

"That isn't funny, Heidi," she said. Oh, but it was. The woman who relished causing chaos with me and my Turkey Dog was finally getting a taste of her own medicine — until a few weeks later when the joke would be on me.

A MONTH after Limerick's arrival, we decided the time had come for the two Turkey Dogs to meet. Mom insisted we introduce them on neutral territory, so we settled for the tennis courts in her neighborhood. Ernie and I arrived first.

As Limerick and Grandmummy came around the corner, I tightened the hold on Ernie's leash.

"Hold on tight to the leash," called Mom as she tightened her own grip.

"Mom, they're fine."

"Heidi, I don't need any more drama. Hold tight to Ernie," she said as they approached us. Ernie seemed oblivious as he was too busy surveying the tennis court for abandoned balls. Limerick lumbered towards us with his ears fanning out to both sides.

"Mom, relax. Geesh. Look, they are going to be fine."

She stopped and looked at me from ten feet away.

"Relax? Do you know what I have been through with this dog? Relax?"

"Stop getting upset. You're going to get the dogs upset."

She furrowed her brow and looked down at Limmy, who led her calmly to where we were standing. The two dogs looked at each other, bumped noses to sniff, and then walked onto the tennis court.

"That was uneventful," I shrugged. I'm not sure what we were expecting as golden retrievers are known for their friendly dispositions. However, I have to admit that I understood why Mom expected a little more excitement from the two mischief makers.

The two spent the next hour sniffing the perimeter of the court, chasing tennis balls, and wagging their tails. We did make one sad discovery during this play session. Limerick didn't know what to do with a ball. When it whizzed by his head, he ran the other way, skipped about, and looked to Ernie for guidance. Thankfully, he was in the presence of a master. Having spent the last year perfecting the finer art of fetch, Ernie trained his new student. I threw the ball in his direction. He let it bounce once and then effortlessly caught it midair. He turned to watch as I threw the ball for Limerick. Sadly, the athletic artistry I witnessed during the couch christening did not appear on the tennis court. He tripped over his feet while attempting to pirouette and catch the ball. It continued to bounce until he finally caught it underneath his paw and scooped it into his mouth. He looked to Ernie for approval. By the end of the session, Limmy had caught the ball in his mouth a few times. Ernie still had a lot to teach him, but we were making progress. After a while, we trotted them back to the house for water and treats.

As Mom and I sat on the couch watching the two dogs sleep side-by-side, I turned to her.

"See. They're fine," I said. "Bring Limerick to my house next time."

"Oh, I don't know..."

"Mom, don't be paranoid!"

MOM RELENTED, and their next play date occurred at my house. Just as before, the initial greeting proved to be uneventful. Limerick marched through the front door while Ernie looked on.

"See! Nothing to worry about," I smirked at Mom. It was fun to prove her wrong.

Moments later, the calmness subsided as a tornado of activity ensued. Down came the fake ficus tree in my living room. Smash went the pot holding the hydrangeas. Charlie and Annie leapt for the safety of the couch as the two Turkey Dogs exploded into a friendly wrestling match that left every piece of furniture at risk. Once the initial shock subsided, Mom and I settled down to watch the two wrestle and play. Every now and then, they would pause and clean each other's snouts, but then the shenanigans would begin again. Ernie enjoyed meeting other dogs, but his attention waned shortly after the greeting. He seemed to be an introvert as dogs go, but Limmy the extrovert had piqued his interest. He watched with obvious curiosity as Limmy broke rules that even Ernie hadn't dared to challenge — like knocking over indoor trees.

Mom and I were pleased with their obvious friendship and vowed that we would unite the two on a regular basis. That is when March 15, 2019, a day that will live in infamy, occurred.

THE PHONE RANG, and Mom's picture appeared on my caller ID.

"Heidi?" She was distraught.

"What's wrong?"

"I...I...I...broke my wrist!"

"What? How?"

"I was walking Limmy and I turned to wave at the neighbor and I stepped wrong and I hit the curb and I went to catch myself and it's my right wrist and I don't know what I'm going to do!"

"Mom, did you go to the doctor, or do you need me to take you?"

"No, the neighbor took me."

"Okay, I'll come down to help you and get Limerick. I can watch him for a bit until you can take care of him."

When I arrived, I found Mom nursing her bandaged wrist and crying as she tried to prepare an overnight bag for Limerick. I consoled her the best that I could, but my tenderness evaporated when I saw the instructions she had written shakily with her left hand. I am going to include them here — verbatim.

INSTRUCTIONS FOR LIMMY

AM - Out to potty as soon as get up. Usually does poopie.

7:00-7:30am - Feed 1 container (3 scoops); Give 1/2 container and wait approximately 5 minutes then give rest of container.

*Give 1 Tylosin capsule wrapped in sweet potato then give rest of the container of food.

8:00am - Out to potty

10:00am - Out to potty

Approximately 11:30A-12N - Feed 1 container (3 scoops); Give 1/2 container and wait approximately 5 minutes then give rest of container. Sprinkle the probiotic on his food and mix it up well.

12:00pm - Out to potty

3:30-4pm. - Feed 1 container (TWO scoops); Give 1/2 container and wait approximately 5 minutes then give rest of container. Out to potty after eating.

6pm - Out to potty

7:00-7:30pm - Feed 1 container (3 scoops); Give 1/2 container and wait approximately 5 minutes then give rest of container.

*Give 1 Tylosin capsule wrapped in sweet potato then give the rest of the container of food.

Out to potty after eating.

10:00-11:00pm - Out to potty. Usually does poopie late at night.

"Mother, are you kidding me? The instructions for the Apollo Moon Landing were less complicated than this!"

"Heidi, he has a sensitive tummy. He ate nothing but

garbage on the streets, and you know the trouble I had with him when I first got him. Oh, and don't forget to moisten his food and warm it up in the microwave for ten seconds before you feed it to him. He likes it warm. Don't go over ten seconds because it will be too hot. Under ten seconds is too cold. Just do ten seconds. And, be sure to use a fork to chop it up; otherwise he wolfs it down and then he gets sick."

I looked down at Limerick. I thought I was taking home a four-year-old golden retriever, but this seemed more like a geriatric patient making one last futile attempt to survive. Sighing, I grabbed Limmy's overnight bag and leash.

When we got to my house, Ernie greeted us, and Limmy made himself at home on the couch. Within moments, he was sound asleep. The excitement of the day and his new surroundings exhausted him, so Ernie and I settled in for the night. We were grateful for a quiet evening of Hallmark movies and cold pizza.

Our peace did not last long.

A WET TONGUE swiped across my face at 5:02 a.m. the following morning. I opened one eye to find a golden retriever scrunching up his nose to flash his "smile" at me.

"Limmy, it's not time yet. Go back to sleep," I urged, burying my face in the pillow. This only excited him more. His entire body convulsed, and he began to whine. Ernie, still snoring on his bed, ignored it all.

"Limerick, go to sleep." The sixty-pound retriever took this as an invitation to join me in bed. With no room left for me, I groaned and rolled out of my warm cocoon.

I fed Limerick, started the coffeepot, and looked back into the bedroom. Ernie, Annie, and Charlie continued to sleep soundly. I spent the next hour eating my oatmeal as an energetic Turkey Dog waited anxiously for his playmate to join him.

An hour later, Ernie and the cats walked out, yawning and bleary-eyed. Limerick dashed over to greet them, but none of them were ready for the furry tornado barreling towards them. Annie and Charlie once again leapt onto the couch while Ernie ignored the nips at his feet, urging him to play. Once I fed Ernie and had my morning coffee, I opened the back door and let the dogs onto the patio to play. Ernie spent the time searching for peanut shells that the squirrels left behind, while Limmy mimicked his actions. Convinced that this would entertain them for a while, I returned to the Coffeemaker to refill my cup.

As I started to settle on the couch, I looked outside and saw Ernie still sniffing the ground, but Limerick was nowhere to be found. I ran to the door and threw it open. At the far corner of the fence that separates my yard from my neighbors, dirt and mud were spewing into the air as Limerick pawed at the ground determined to dig an escape route.

"Limerick! Stop that!" I yelled. He did and came running over to me, proud of his accomplishment. The once cream dog now resembled a chocolate lab.

"Are you kidding me? Now you need a bath." He sat back and looked up with a toothy grin. "No, this is not funny. I just want to drink my coffee."

After I cleaned him off and refilled the hole in my backyard, I sat down for my now cold cup of java. I was only a few sips in when I looked outside and saw my ornamental pine tree moving across the back patio. Bolting for the door again, I threw it open to find Limerick had not only uprooted the tree, but he was now dragging it across the yard. Let me state that again in case you didn't fully understand: the "sweet, calm" Limerick we had been promised had just uprooted an entire pine tree and was now dragging it across the patio.

The next few days continued in a similar fashion. The ficus tree in my living room remained a casualty of countless wrestling matches. More large holes appeared in the backyard. A pair of headphones met their demise after being mistaken for a chew toy. A baby gate used to protect the cats' food came crashing down. Pillows flew off the couch. Toys littered the floor, and counter surfing became a new addition to mealtime.

As the chaos ensued, Ernie Bert began to unveil even more of a mischievous side of himself. He didn't always partake in Limerick's naughtiness, but he certainly watched with a look of admiration. He continued to teach Limmy how to fetch while he learned the finer art of takedowns and headlocks.

At night, the two finally settled down, exhausted from their day of play. Limerick would stretch his entire frame across two dog beds while Ernie found a cold, hard place on the floor beside him. If Ernie slept on the couch next to me, Limerick would launch himself over the coffee table to land in between the two of us. That said, there were several times when I came home to find the two snuggling on the couch or waiting side by side at the front door with tails wagging and cold noses fogging up the window.

In every relationship, there are tests that challenge the strength of the bond. Three weeks later, Limerick tested this bond in a unique way.

~

I FINALLY LOST my cool on a particularly stressful day when I raced home during my morning break to let the dogs out. I had been trying my best to adhere to Grandmummy's geriatric schedule for her nimble canine. I only had forty minutes to spare before I had to be back at school for cafeteria patrol. With a thirty-minute round trip commute, it left a mere ten minutes to let the dogs out and feed both of them. When I pulled into the driveway, I was surprised to only see Limerick standing at the window, wagging his tail.

"Hello, sweet boy! Where's Ernie?" I asked as I reached down to pet Limmy. Spreading his mouth into a wide smile, I saw that Jed Clampett had returned. Instead of birdseed, his pearly whites were now covered in a chocolate goo and aluminum foil. He tore into the dining room and proudly stood over an empty box of Viactiv with four untouched supplements still lying on the floor.

"Limmy! What have you done?" I yelled as he lunged for the remaining supplements. I grabbed them out of his reach and opened his mouth to see if I could save any others from the bowels of the Turkish Tweety.

"Where's Ernie?" I cried in a panic. I ran into the living room and found him lying on the couch with an "I-told-him-not-to-do-it-but-he-wouldn't-listen" look on his face. His expressive eyebrows jumped back and forth as he watched the scene unfold. After a frantic call to the vet, I loaded Limmy into the car and raced to the clinic to have his stomach pumped. The calcium and chocolate levels in the supplement could be fatal for dogs, so I knew every minute counted. I stepped on the accelerator and prayed that I wouldn't pass a police officer as I sped to the clinic. Halfway there, it donned on me I hadn't checked Ernie's mouth to see if he had eaten anything. I screeched into the parking lot, slammed the car in park, and flung open the door.

"Limmy, let's go!" I commanded as I jumped out. I raced into the lobby and announced, "We're here! I need to go get Ernie."

The front desk associate took the leash from my hand and raced Limerick to the back.

"Please be okay," I prayed as I sped home to get Ernie.

Without detailing the chocolaty goo and tinsel contents of Limmy's stomach, let me just say this: we got lucky. Really lucky. Both dogs were fine despite Limerick eating the entire box of Viactiv. As suspected, Ernie ate none.

After blood tests, charcoal treatments to induce vomiting, emergency vet bills, and boarding costs, I returned to the vet clinic to find a $1500 bill and two golden retrievers — one smiling and the other one sulking, rightfully so. I also received a bag containing Limmy's flea and tick medication. On the front of the orange bag, the technician had written in big letters "Best Dog Ever!" My jaw dropped. In six short months, Limerick had marked every piece of furniture in sight, uprooted a pine tree, knocked over a ficus tree, broken several baby gates, hogged the couch and dog beds, racked up a $1500 vet bill, eaten a box of Viactiv, downed a birdseed bell, and caused Ernie to have his stomach pumped. Best dog ever?!?! Were they crazy? More like "Best *Worst* Dog Ever!"

I glared down into the chestnut brown eyes staring up at me. And then Limerick did what he does best. He smiled.

LIMERICK CONTINUED to flash his golden grin whenever he found trouble for Ernie and him to get into. The Facebook fans loved Ernie's naughty sidekick and his mischief making. After a while, I began to relax and find humor in his antics, too. After four months with the birdseed bandit, I also thought I had finally Turkey Dogged the house, but I was wrong. He no longer wanted bird seed or calcium chews. Now he was after cat litter.

I returned home one night to find Annie sitting primly next to Charlie on the back of the couch. The two did not greet me at the door with the dogs like they normally did. Annie had a disturbed look on her face, and Charlie looked back at me through slanted eyes. Something was wrong.

I looked towards the laundry room that held their litter box and saw a trail of cat litter leading into the guest bathroom that housed their food. Limerick had struck again.

Every baby gate I put up, Limerick knocked down or squeezed through. At one point, I was so flummoxed by how he was getting into the cat litter I staked out the baby gate leading into the cats' area. When he thought I wasn't looking, I watched as he slinked his sixty-pound body through a four-inch by eight-inch opening for the cats to walk through. It was the same athleticism I had witnessed when he first arrived in America. It was then that I realized I was in the presence of greatness. Once I barricaded the entrance with two baby gates, two chairs, a wooden box, and some duct tape, I spent the rest of the day trying to find the phone number for the head coach of the USA Olympic Team. Clearly, I had a candidate for their gymnastics program.

Several months later, Limerick returned to Grandmummy's home, and I have to admit that despite all of his troublemaking, I spent several nights crying myself to sleep. Yes, I knew I would get to see him regularly, but I missed the rapscallion and the excitement he brought to our household. He was a wonderful distraction to the stressors of life, and he certainly made each day interesting. Most importantly, he reminded me that no matter how crazy life becomes, no matter how many storm clouds seem to get in my way, I can always do one thing to make the day better — smile.

18

MR. ERNIE BERT GOES TO
WASHINGTON

Springtime in Washington, D.C., is beautiful. The city is aglow with a soft light that accentuates every statue, and there is a feeling of newness and rebirth that energizes the masses. Pink cherry blossoms dance in the breeze, and iPhones click to record special moments in front of the many scenic walkways and waterways. Despite its loveliness, springtime is not the time to take a Turkey Dog to the nation's capital. Once again, I learned the hard way.

After a year in the United States, Grandmummy and I decided it was time for Ernie's rescuers to see his progress. He now had a thick coat of fur, and his limp had become virtually undetectable. We had always wanted to see the cherry blossoms in bloom, so we planned a lunch reunion with Fairy Godmother, Michelle, and Chari.

Prior to meeting them, we planned to take Ernie to most of the historical sights: the White House, Washington Monument, Capitol, and the Smithsonian. On the drive up, I envisioned a day full of epic photo moments complete with historic monuments and scenic vistas for his Facebook page. However, what we found were massive crowds of tourists fighting for the chance to stand in front of the same backdrops.

Undeterred, Ernie Bert, Grandmummy, and I muscled our way through the crowds and snapped a few photographs of our own in front of the White House. Wearing an Old Glory hat, Ernie posed with the D.C. Police. Mom and I beamed with pride, yet once again, Ernie acted bored and unimpressed. He found the fire hydrants more to his liking than a crowded walkway where no one paid attention to him.

Still determined to catch the perfect photo moment for his Facebook fans, I made it our goal to walk to the Capitol and have Ernie Bert pose on the white marble steps. This image could propel us into the next stratosphere of social media stardom. I envisioned a grassroots movement to elect him President and secure my role as First Mother. I set our compass to the marble steps and looked eastward.

As we ambled that way, I remained impressed by Ernie's focus and stamina. Although the smells distracted him, he continued to be most cooperative. We maintained a brisk pace since we had one hour to get to the Capitol and take the picture before we had to meet Fairy Godmother, Chari, and Michelle. Maneuvering our way to the front of the White House, we rounded the corner to run smack into our first obstacle: Japanese tourists. I did not realize that the American cherry blossom festivities would be interesting for those whose country gifted the trees to ours many years ago. I also did not realize the adoration that Japanese women have for golden retrievers. I was even more surprised by the degree of showmanship Ernie could produce when surrounded by a bevy of beautiful women. My bored and obedient Turkey Dog turned on the suave and immediately charmed his new admirers. With five women stroking his belly and cooing at him, my dog became an international sex symbol right before my eyes.

He rolled over on his back and let the ladies pose with him and whisper sweet nothings into his ear. Drunk with love, he wiggled from side to side and flipped over a few more times to the gleeful cries of his harem. When I explained he was from Turkey, the choir of "oohs" and "aahs" created even more of a fervor around the furry stud muffin. After nearly ten minutes of SnapChat videos, Instagram posts, and Facebook Live sessions, I tried to extract Ernie from his fan club. My efforts were successful, but only for a few minutes. As we approached the Lawn, another group of Japanese tourists stopped and begged us for pictures. It soon became apparent that a picture at the Capitol would have to wait. Ernie's public needed him, and he did not want to disappoint.

Once again, he rolled on his back, butted his head against the tourists' legs, and wagged his tail, lapping up every compliment and "handsome boy" sent his way. Looking at our watches, Mom and I agreed we needed to head to the Turkish restaurant where we would meet the rescue staff. Once again, we said goodbye to our new friends and quickly made our way to the car. Actually, by "quickly" I mean that we only allowed Ernie to sniff every other signpost and fire hydrant along the route.

Returning to the car, I realized in all the confusion with the crowds and paparazzi I had never taken a picture of the cherry blossoms. Luckily, there were a few trees in a park close to the car, so we quickly posed on a bench underneath one of the flowering majesties. Then it was off to lunch.

～

In a historic part of D.C. known as Adams Morgan, we met the women who had rescued our street urchin turned sex symbol. Over the course of only a few years, they had rescued nearly five hundred dogs from Turkey. It only seemed appropriate that we should dine at a Turkish restaurant under the sunshine of the nation's capital to celebrate their accomplishments. After the initial kisses and hugs, Ernie Bert seemed exhausted by the estrogen overload, so he lay down on the sidewalk as we chatted and laughed over pizza and Turkish baklava.

Joining us was another Turkey Dog named Dublin. Fairy Godmother had rescued Dublin and fallen in love with him. Dublin has a rich brown and red coat that complements his Irish name. However, he has the sass and spunk of a Turkey Dog. For instance, if he is left alone in the car to wait for Fairy Godmother to finish an errand, he will do so until he runs out of patience. At that time, he will climb into the driver's seat and lay on the horn until his human heeds his call.

Dublin showed this same Turkey Dog chutzpah during our lunch. As the wine flowed and the laughter reached a crescendo, the red-headed canine began to feel ignored. Taking matters into his own hands, he jumped up and listened to our conversation perched high atop the table behind us.

"He's part mountain goat," Fairy Godmother explained as she turned to see what had caught our attention. She continued with her story, and Dublin placed his snout in between her and Michelle to listen intently.

After more than two hours of stories, delicious food, and laughter, the time came to depart. Ernie barked his desire to return home, and Dublin joined suit. With a few more hugs and photos, our adventure in D.C. had come to an end.

On the drive home, Ernie snored in the backseat while Mom and I chatted about the fun day. After recounting our new memories, she turned to me with a smile creasing the corners of her mouth.

"You know what, Heidi? Fairy Godmother, Chari, and Michelle...they seem like...well...they seem like family, don't they?"

"Yes. Yes, they do."

$\approx$

A FEW DAYS after our trip to the nation's capital, Mom called an emergency family meeting at my house. She refused to tell us what it was in reference to, so Gretchen and I sat nervously at the dining room table, waiting for her arrival.

The front door opened, and Mom strolled in with a yellow legal pad in one hand and her purse in the other. She greeted Ernie and the cats and nonchalantly sat down at the table.

"Girls, how are you?"

"Mom, what is going on?" I asked anxiously.

"Oh, your place looks great, Heidi. I like where you put Muckie's china cabinet," she said, looking at the family heirlooms that decorated the glass cabinet. My beloved grandmother had passed away several months prior after living a long and happy life. Since Mom was an only child, she had divided the keepsakes between herself, Gretchen, and me.

"Yes, thanks. Mom, what's wrong?" I asked again.

"Nothing," she smiled. "I've...I've been thinking." With that, she placed the legal pad on the table, and I saw it contained pages of notations.

"Okay..." I said looking at Gretchen. She appeared just as puzzled and worried as me.

"Girls, your grandparents left me a generous inheritance, and I want to talk to you about it."

"Okay," I said, still not sure where this was going.

"My parents loved animals, and Bobby always believed in giving back. I want to use this money for good, but I want your permission. This money is your inheritance, too. When I'm gone, you'll receive the rest, so I want to make sure that you are okay with what I'm going to propose."

Gretchen and I glanced quickly at each other.

"I'd like to donate a sizable portion to help the Turkey Dogs," she said, looking at each of us. "I did the math, and I think if we donate this amount, we can pay the cost for at least fifteen dogs to come to America and find new homes." She pointed to a figure on the paper. I looked at it and smiled excited by the notion.

"Fairy Godmother, Chari, and Michelle work so hard to help those dogs, and look at the magic they create for so many families. Just look at what it has done for our family," she continued. She spent the next few minutes detailing her idea and ways in which the money could be used. When she was done, she sat back, waiting for our opinions.

"I love the idea!" Gretchen said, practically bouncing in her seat. Mom looked at me.

"Heidi, what do you think?"

"Yes. One hundred times, yes. Thank you, Mom, thank you so much!" I cried as I reached over to hug her. "Muckie and Bobby would be so proud of you, Mom."

"Well, Bobby worked so hard to provide for us, so I want to make sure that we use this money wisely. I can't think of a better organization to do that with."

Shortly thereafter, Mom's donation arrived. Through

thoughtful and strategic planning, the women were able to rescue sixty-three dogs with the money — nearly quadruple the amount we had anticipated. The rescued goldens became known as the Speece Dogs, and with each new adoption, we received updates and thank-you notes from the new owners. Mom read each letter and email numerous times, and Gretchen and I created a scrapbook to keep track of each dog and its story. There was a Truman in Pennsylvania, an Ike in Virginia Beach, a Dior in D.C., and a Pippa in Maryland just to name a few. With each rescue, we added new members to our growing extended family.

They say that if you want to meet people, get a dog. "They" are right. In a matter of months, our family of three became a family of several hundred. New friends and old friends entered our lives or became reacquainted through Ernie's Facebook page. We continued to have reunions when families vacationed in our area or during annual picnics and get-togethers. We exchanged Christmas cards and birthday wishes.

Through this experience, I learned that family is what you make it. We may not share a bloodline, but we do share a love for golden retrievers. This bond and the kindness that embodies our golden community is one that can only be described as family.

No, I didn't get my big Italian family, but I may have found something even better. Thanks to Ernie Bert and Mom's generosity, I found a community that loves animals as much as I do. We share in the joy of each new adoption and hold each other up during the loss of a furry loved one. We celebrate milestones together and look forward to yearly reunions. It may not be as exciting as the Italian mob, but it is rather nice not having to look over my shoulder every time I leave the pizza parlor.

19

POMP AND CIRCUMSTANCE

People around the world celebrate New Year's Eve as the beginning of something wonderful and full of promise. Teachers have their own New Year's Eve; it's called "The Last Day of School." As the final essay is dissected with a red pen, and the last moldy locker remnants find their way to the trash, teachers begin to pack up their rooms and celebrate a life without bells, meetings, and emails. A sense of anticipation fills the air, and the teachers and students find a renewed energy and optimism to propel them through the final days of classes and exams. Birds return to chirping, and the sun reappears as young and old look forward to a much-needed break from each other.

Before this break can begin, though, an important rite of passage known as graduation occurs. It's a day full of pomp, accolades, and speeches—lots of speeches. That summer, my students voted to have me give one of the convocation addresses. This is an incredible honor and responsibility for any individual; and it was especially so for me. I had grown close to a number of students in the class, and I knew I would miss seeing them in the halls the following year. These would be the last words that many would ever hear from me as they embarked on their new lives. What do I say? Do I talk about my past foibles? Do I spew motivational quotes at them? Do I lecture? Inspire? Entertain? I spent countless hours writing motivational messages, only to scrap them the next day. I knew what I wanted to convey, but I didn't know how.

And then I thought of Mom and her donation. And I thought of Ernie and the lessons he had taught me. In under three minutes, I delivered the following message:

GRADUATION DAY. *Many of you never thought it would come, but here it is. After four long years of blood, sweat, tears, frantic phone calls home to Mom, and numerous therapy sessions curled up in the guidance counselor's office crying, "Is this the meaning of life!?!?"...it is now time to celebrate. Congratulations, TEACHERS! We did it!*

Graduates, congrats to you, too.

In all seriousness, thank you for this unique opportunity to talk to you one last time before you embark on a new adventure.

Since I can't pay off your student loans, I'm going to let you in on a little secret. Of all of the classes you took, of all of the hours you spent studying late at night, there is one discipline that ranks above the others. You may think I'm going to say English, but you are wrong. The discipline that is the most important and the one that I hope you continue to study regardless of your future profession is history.

If you don't know where you come from, how do you know where you are going? Unfortunately, many people of your age do not recognize this simple fact. Instead, pop culture dictates you should "Live in the Moment," "Celebrate Yourself," and "Let You be You." In this self-help and selfie society, we tend to forget the hundreds of lives before us and around us that made this graduation day possible. We wouldn't be here today if it wasn't for the soldier who stormed the beaches at Normandy. The woman who worked tirelessly in a sweatshop trying to create a better life for her children. The distant relative who gave up everything in hopes of achieving the American Dream. The police officer who keeps us safe at night. The nurse who leaves her family to work a 24-hour shift to comfort the sick. And the countless others who devoted their lives to serving a cause bigger than themselves.

Yes, today is special. Most of you worked very hard to get here. However, so did 3.6 million other teenagers around the nation who are graduating this year. What makes you different from them? Nothing...yet. The "yet" is all up to you.

Ben Franklin used to ask himself every morning "What good will I do today?" At night, he would ask "What good have I done today?" Will you do the same?

Here is my challenge, graduates: dedicate yourself to something bigger than yourself. Put away the phones. Put away the selfies, and look outside yourself. When our Founding Fathers wrote "life, liberty, and the pursuit of happiness," they did not mean self-happiness. They meant the happiness of your community. The happiness of your neighborhood. The happiness of your family. The happiness of your fellow Americans.

Today is most definitely a special day, so enjoy it. Celebrate your accomplishments. But, don't forget to thank the family, friends, teachers, police officers, firefighters, soldiers, nurses, ministers, community leaders, ancestors, and countless others who helped get you on this stage.

And tomorrow. Wake up and ask yourself, "What good will I do today?"

20

LOVE IN THE TIME OF CORONA

"Hello?" I whispered, still trying to understand why my private landline was ringing in the wee hours of the morning.

"Is this the Speece home?" a woman asked.

"Yes."

"Is Janeen Speece there?"

"Who?"

"Janeen Speece. I think I said that correctly. Maybe Jayneen? This is the Indianapolis Alarm Company for Correction Services."

"I'm sorry. What?"

"We're an alarm company for the corrections office. Why have you removed your ankle bracelet?"

"What?!"

"Ma'am, do you or anyone in your household wear an ankle bracelet?" asked the woman on the other end.

"No!"

"Are you sure?"

"Yes!"

"We're sorry to have bothered you. Good night."

THAT WAS MAY 28, 2020. Although I wasn't under house arrest, I was in lockdown thanks to the COVID-19 virus. Somehow the two—house arrest and lockdown—seemed quite similar. Two months prior to that call, the governor of Virginia closed schools, and I found myself at home learning how to work full time with a Turkey Dog constantly at my side. I'm sure in his mind he thought the entire world shut down to accommodate his fetch habit, but I still had bills to pay and a desire to stay employed. Therefore, we had to come to a compromise.

At first, I thought the lockdown was a welcome relief from society and the pressures of my job. Although I have extroverted tendencies, I am really an introvert at heart, like Ernie. The thought of being forced to stay at home with my pets and hobbies seemed like a gift from above. I no longer had to sit in boring staff meetings that often became political. I no longer had to worry about organizing three major work events in one month. I no longer had to look in the mirror before showing up for class. As long as I had on a nice blouse, I could get away with sweatpants or running shorts on the bottom half. Makeup became a thing of the past. Use a filter, and SHAZAM! I was ready to go.

Life seemed grand. I ordered an indoor bike, signed up for the Peloton app, and lost five pounds in the first month. I was ready to rock this lockdown.

Ernie was equally excited and confused. At first, he couldn't understand why I was home all the time, but after a few days, he treated it like a gift. This meant more walks, more treats, and more attention. Every morning, we either walked to the neighborhood dog park that was rarely occupied or the local baseball park that always promised a new ball for the orphanage. When we'd return, we'd promptly feed the squirrels a handful of peanuts and begin work for the day. Ernie curled up on his bed, exhausted from his morning exercise, and I lounged on the couch to make a daily task list. I still couldn't completely give up my "to do" lists.

That said, the quarantine did present a few scheduling challenges for both of us. On a typical day, Ernie naps until his midday feeding. This was understandable until he realized I was now home all the time. This meant that he expected more treats more often. I suspected that this would not only be detrimental to his health, but it would also be detrimental to my online instruction. He proved my suspicions correct. During my first online class of the pandemic, he barked incessantly until I allowed him to go outside and chase the squirrels. Not only did this disrupt an important lesson on the literary devices in *The Things They Carried*—a pivotal, life-altering moment—but it also caused many giggles and eye rolls from my teenage audience.

I reminded myself that this new reality was strange for both of us. He was used to having my undivided attention when I was home, and he didn't realize that now others were expecting the same treatment. I ignored his poor behavior until I couldn't anymore. After he belched loudly, dropped Mr. Ballie on the keyboard, and groaned off screen, causing one teenage hooligan to ask if I had porn on in the background, I decided it was time that we have a "chat."

"Ernie, we need to talk," I said as he eyed me uncertainly. "Do you see this? This roof, this couch, this fireplace, this home. All the things you love and make you comfortable?"

He blinked.

"Ernie, these all cost money. In order to get that money, I can't spend every waking moment with you. During normal times, Mom would be at work teaching students important lessons about Edgar Allan Poe and Henry Wadsworth Longfellow. Things that will determine their future. Now, I have to do that from home, so I need your cooperation. I need you to be quiet and good while I'm online talking to my students. When I'm done working, I promise to focus my attention on you. Do you understand? Can we agree to that arrangement?"

He blinked again, refusing to commit. Then he yawned and let out another belch. Clearly, I had struck a chord.

The next few lessons went by without disruption. Ernie snored at my side, but my students didn't seem to hear or notice. After I logged off, I awarded him with a walk to the baseball field. Along the way, we made new discoveries. We found a hidden gazebo surrounded by hundred-year-old maple trees in a neighboring community. We came upon a private lookout for a scenic river view and watched as sailboats passed by. We traversed abandoned homesteads from the 1700s and hiked through historic battlefields. At night, we found another relaxing rhythm: popcorn and love stories thanks to the Hallmark Channel. Yes, lockdown life was ideal—until it wasn't.

Towards the end of the second month, I began to crumble. I missed my students, but I desperately needed to divorce myself from technology. One thing that the pandemic illuminated is that online fatigue is real and dangerous. After spending too much time in video conferences, one can become depressed, anxious, and exhausted. I found this to be true. Some may say that I should be grateful to be employed during this time, and I wholeheartedly agree. I was lucky. However, it didn't come without its challenges.

Not only did I find myself exhausted by the end of each day, but I also became irritable and unhealthy. I was no longer in a regular routine, and I had to navigate new terrain. As much as I don't want to admit it, I find comfort in routine. Now the day could be redesigned in a number of unfamiliar ways. What did I make for dinner since I couldn't order out? Did I exercise in the morning or in the afternoon? After spending all day on technology, could I ignore the call from a friend, or did I need to return it right away? To wash the hair or not wash the hair? Those were the questions. In the big scheme of things, they were minor inconveniences. However, in my tiny world, they were monumental, and they led to a breaking point.

After eight weeks of wearing a mask, watching countless news reports, conversing with friends and colleagues online, avoiding Mom and Gretchen to protect them, giving in to every Ernie whim, washing my hands until they were raw, and becoming acutely aware of a six-foot radius around my being, I broke. I mean I BROKE! I cried, and I cried, and I cried. I had nightmares and woke up in a sweat, fearing that loved ones had suddenly died. This led to tiresome mornings, which led to eating every sugary treat in sight. Cheese became an endangered species around me. And, I did something that I didn't think was possible: I watched every movie on the Hallmark Channel. When I got to where I was watching former reality stars try to act, I knew that I had hit rock bottom. A hidden virus had become my nemesis and emotional downfall. I had entered the rabbit hole, and I was heading straight for the Mad Hatter's Tea Party. Something had to give. And it did.

~

ONE NIGHT IN JUNE, three months into quarantine and just shy of my forty-fifth birthday, I dusted myself off after another crying session and decided that I needed to make dinner. I threw a handful of peanuts onto the patio for the squirrels to eat, and then Ernie and I plodded into the kitchen to stare into the refrigerator and debate about what I could throw together for a meal. He stared at the smoked salmon, but I didn't have the energy. I settled for a grilled turkey sandwich and warmed up the toaster oven. Disappointed with my decision, Ernie slumped towards the living room.

"Beggars can't be choosers, big guy," I scolded as I piled on the mozzarella cheese. I plopped the questionable formation into the oven and closed the door. Then I focused on the podcast that had been playing in the background. For several months, I had been listening to a natural foods chef and her husband discuss calming ways to approach life. This particular episode dealt with happiness and its definition. It seemed slightly sadistic considering that the only way I was about to celebrate my milestone birthday was with a mask and a safe distance away from my family. Just as I started to become lost in the narrator's story about a real-life *Lord of the Flies*, Ernie let out another loud sigh which signaled that he had lost his patience with me and demanded to be let out immediately. I scolded him for his rudeness, opened the door, and continued to listen to the podcast.

"If we assume most people are selfish and design our societies around that, then that is the type of society we will get," the interviewer said.

"See, Ernie. You should be more grateful," I called to the back door. The toaster oven dinged, and I returned to the kitchen to set the broiler and put the final golden touches on the mozzarella oozing down the sides of my sandwich.

"When in doubt, assume the best in other people because so often we don't really know what the intentions of other people are."

As the toaster oven ticked away and the commentator continued to persuade his audience that true happiness was possible, my shoulders relaxed and my tense jaw loosened. That is when Ernie began to bark ferociously at the back fence.

Ernie barks. Ernie barks a lot. However, he never barks ferociously. This was a new level of intensity that immediately snapped me back to reality. Rabid raccoon? Serial killer?

I sprinted for the back door and ran onto the patio. My happy-go-lucky Turkey Dog stood barking with a viciousness that I had never heard before in a golden retriever.

I sucked in a breath, summoned my courage, and crept up behind him.

"What is it?"

He growled and remained transfixed. His back end started quivering ready to attack.

"Okay. Is it a raccoon?"

"Grrrrrr...." He let out a low rumble from deep inside his belly.

Could it be a coyote? Two years ago, Grandmummy had mourned the loss of her neighborhood goose to the clutches of a coyote, and I had heard that the same hungry animals were prowling neighborhoods in the area. With their forests and woodlands diminished, they had begun haunting the local suburbs in search of food in the form of chickens, house cats, or small dogs. It seemed only natural that the brave and stalwart Ernie Bert would sacrifice his life and limb to protect Annie, Charlie, and his beloved mother.

Just as I was ready to throw a lawn chair over the fence, I saw the true cause of the evening's distress. There on the ground, tucked behind a flower pot and out of his reach, was a peanut. Yes, a peanut. The great and honorable Ernie Bert, descendant of Lord Tweedmouth's Scottish lot, carrier of the Turkish royal lineage, and former street dog had forced me to abandon my dinner for a peanut.

"Grrrrrr..." he rumbled.

I reached down and picked up the nut. Ernie snatched it from my hand and downed the specimen. He let out a satisfied belch, licked his chops, and sauntered back inside satisfied by his hunting expedition. I remained outside alone in the dark staring at the ground where the peanut once lay. Slowly, my heart rate returned to normal, and I turned to follow Ernie inside.

As smoke wafted from my toaster oven, I abandoned my burnt sandwich and settled for a jar of peanut butter and another Hallmark movie with another reality television star. Thank you, COVID-19. This was my life, and I was about to turn forty-five.

"Happy BIRTHHHHHHHDAY, BFF!!!!" cheered a text from a longtime friend as I squinted to read the message from my groggy sleep. It was June 8. Nice sentiment, but my birthday is on June 9. This seemed like a typical 2020 move. Here I was about to mark the halfway point of my life, and even my closest friends couldn't get it right.

With Annie bellowing for her morning meal and Ernie pacing in front of the back door, I willed myself out of bed and looked in the mirror. The old saying was true. People do end up looking like their dogs. Three years ago, Ernie came to me with what his vet called a "tragic face." It is when a golden retriever resembles a Shar-Pei with excessive wrinkles around the brow and jowls. Sometimes malnutrition causes this, but in Ernie's case, it was just Ernie. He used it to his advantage to beg for treats and win Facebook followers. It was adorable on him, but now I had developed my own tragic face. It didn't have the same effect on a middle-aged woman. The sagging neckline had become more prominent. The vertical furrow between my eyes had staked a permanent claim, and my crow's feet looked like the entire cast of *The Birds* had marched across my face. I had become my dog, and my life was half over.

Dejected, I downed my oatmeal and coffee, wishing for the gods to grant me some ambrosia to make it through the next fifteen hours of sunlight. Once again, Ernie paced restlessly, so I found his leash for our morning walk. As I focused on the pavement and disappeared into my thoughts, Ernie led us to the baseball field. He loved visiting as it usually meant that he found a few stray lacrosse balls or baseballs waiting to be rescued. Today was no different.

As I watched him gnaw at the leather casing of the baseball he had discovered, I reflected on my life. Standing in the middle of the field at first base, I stared at the empty scoreboard to my right.

"What exactly have I done with life? What have I really done aside from calling a few bingo games and teaching teenagers about the 'importance' of a book that they probably won't even read?" I asked aloud.

I wasn't really sure. Forty-five years of life gone and nothing to show for it aside from a few stories to entertain coworkers over cocktails. I stared at Ernie lying in the wet grass at my feet. Here was a living being that had survived on the streets, traveled farther than most dogs in the world, acclimatized to a new culture and country, and brought joy to everyone he met. He didn't have a formal education or a formal career, yet he seemed to accomplish more than me on a daily basis. There in the middle of the field, staring at an empty scoreboard, I began to cry.

THE FOLLOWING MORNING, June 9, I found myself once again standing in the middle of the baseball diamond while my Turkey Dog celebrated the newest addition to his orphanage. The phone rang, and I braced myself for another call from the Indianapolis Correction Services operator.

"Happy birthday to you! Happy birthday to you! Happy birthday, dear Heidi! Happy birthday to you!" It was Mom and not a prison warden.

"Thanks, Mom," I said, feigning happiness. "At least I'm forty-five and halfway done with this crazy world."

"What?" she asked.

"I said 'I'm forty-five, so my life is halfway over.'"

"What do you mean you're forty-five? You're forty-four!"

"Huh?"

"You're forty-four."

"No, I'm not. I'm..."

Wait a minute. I did the math in my head, and then it

dawned on me. I *was* forty-four! In one night, I had been gifted an entire year. A gift of 365 days. My life *wasn't* half over. Was this possible?

As soon as I got off the phone, I started making a mental list of all the things I was going to do with my new year. Calligraphy classes. Learn Italian. Start my own business. Create a website. Start a blog. Learn photography. Master the art of cooking. Lose ten pounds. Run a virtual 5K. Read a book each week. Learn how to meditate. Take an online course. Start an Etsy shop. Expand Ernie's Facebook page. Paint the house. Landscape the yard.

And then my eyes fell on Ernie. He now lay in the grass on his back, soaking up the morning sunshine. The baseball sat beside him as he watched a bird fly overhead. His pink belly moved up and down as he breathed in the warm summer air. As I watched him, I had an epiphany. The time had come to let go of the "to do" list and the unrealistic expectations. Maybe I would learn a new language or start a new hobby, but I wasn't going to force myself to do it because of some arbitrary list. For the first time in my life, I gave myself permission to relax my standards and let life happen organically.

I sat down beside Ernie in the grass and looked up to watch the birds along with him. Three years had passed since he had entered my life, and I thought back to all the lessons he had taught me along the way.

Golden retrievers, especially rescued ones, have an uncanny understanding of the world. They know evil exists, but they treat each person, animal, and opportunity as if it is a birthday gift or a new ball. Until they are given a reason to believe otherwise, they embrace everything with a happy heart and an infectious smile. When they are in pain, they don't show it. They simply plod along and look for the joy in the situation. If it is a bone on a doctor's table, a scrap of food from a kind stranger, or a fetch session in the backyard, they find happiness in the simple things. Ernie Bert has mastered this. Instead of worrying about the future or harboring resentment for past wrongs, he pursues his passion with abandon and demands that the world accept him, quirks and all. Like so many dogs, he only requires five things — food, water, shelter, belly rubs, and Mr. Ballie. No costumes, no elaborate resumes, no honorary degrees, no Facebook likes. Just good old-fashioned love, family, friends, and purpose.

When I talk to other dog owners, they express the same mysticism. How can these creatures that can't speak, make laws, or find the cure for cancer create so much healing and happiness in the world? If they can do it, why can't human beings do it?

In fact, that might be the greatest lesson Ernie Bert has taught me. Sometimes the quietest impact makes the greatest noise. Ernie entered my life in an IKEA parking lot. There was nothing glamorous about it. No fame. No pomp. No circumstance. Nothing. However, the impact that his entrance has made on my life and many others is deafening.

Every morning, he greets me with a bark and a smile. He then runs out of the room, throws Mr. Ballie in the air, and embraces the day with a sense of adventure and optimism. At night, he curls up, content knowing that once again he has enriched my life and fulfilled his purpose.

As I stroked his belly, he rolled to his side and looked up at me.

"Thank you, Ernie Bert. I love you, big guy."

With a grunt, he stood up and took the baseball in his mouth. It was time to return home and introduce his new friend to Mr. Ballie and the rest of his orphanage. As we arrived at the front door, Ernie plopped the baseball on the stoop and looked up at me.

"Guess what?" I asked. His eyebrows danced from side to side.

"We just gained another 365 days of fetch time together!" He broke into a big golden grin, barked twice, picked up his new toy, and walked inside. Day one had just begun.

Happy Memories

Grandmummy and Ernie

Bringing Ernie home

Limerick

Some of his orphans

Naptime with Mr. Ballie

Obedience School

SPEECENOTES

As a high school English teacher, I am quite familiar with SparkNotes, CliffNotes, Shmoop, and other websites aimed at giving the teenage mind a condensed and watered-down version of a complex piece of literature. I am not a purist; I actually see the benefit in using such tools to enhance the experience. The character breakdowns, plot overviews, and setting descriptions can help a young learner when tackling the likes of *Wuthering Heights* or *The Scarlet Letter*.

Therefore, since I fully expect this book to find its rightful place with the other great classics, whether that is on a bookshelf or under a wobbly table leg, I have included my version in the form of SpeeceNotes. Feel free to highlight certain passages or make a cheat sheet on the palm of your hand.

MAIN CHARACTERS

ERNIE BERT *(also known as Ernie, Big Guy, and Mr. Love Monkey)* - golden retriever from Istanbul, Turkey, who serves as the protagonist of this story. Ernie Bert is wise beyond his dog years. A woman discovered him malnourished, unkempt, and suffering from an injured hip outside of an Istanbul auto body shop in 2017. Arriving in America on July 4, 2017, his bumbling human, Heidi, adopted him the following day. Known to be mischievous and independent, he lives by the motto "I am what I am."

HEIDI - ERNIE BERT'S human. After growing up in small-town Nebraska and holding several prestigious jobs as a bingo caller, line dance instructor, Christmas elf, and napkin folder, she went back to school and became a teacher. After more than ten years of teaching in a high school classroom, she adopted Ernie and realized that the tables had turned. She had become the student.

MOM (ALSO KNOWN as Grandmummy) - Ernie Bert's grandmother and Heidi's mother. Grandmummy is a strong, honorable, and opinionated woman who often sides with Ernie Bert. She spoils him with toys that she knows will annoy her daughter, and her sociopathic tendencies are likely due to years spent isolated in Nebraska. Despite her devious side, Grandmummy is an avid animal advocate who has helped save countless lives due to her generosity and giant heart.

GRETCHEN (ALSO KNOWN as Auntie G) - Ernie Bert's aunt and Heidi's sister. Auntie G is a rule follower, and many are surprised to learn that she and Heidi are even sisters. She is tall; Heidi is short. She has brown hair and green eyes; Heidi has blonde hair and blue eyes. She prefers to stay at home; Heidi loves to travel. Although they come from the same womb, they are two very different women. Gretchen is also the type of person who will happily give you her first-born child if she thought you truly wanted it. She would then ask you if you needed help raising the child or if you would like her to fund his/her college education. When you said "yes" because you planned to use the funds to hit the Nordstrom sales rack, she would then offer to sell her kidney on the black market to ensure you had enough for Harvard and a new pair of Jimmy Choos.

CHARLIE - THE PATRIARCH of the Speece Family and brother of Ernie. Charlie is a sixteen-year-old tuxedo cat from the Broward County SPCA. He is a handsome fellow and is always dressed to impress. Although Charlie has grown to accept Ernie, he refuses to give up his throne and has an unbelievable ability to sleep through the chaos. This is most likely because of his catnip addiction.

ANNIE - THE DIVA of the Speece Family and Ernie's sister. Annie is an orange rescue kitty from Johnstown, Pennsylvania. Her rescuers found her trying to survive outside in the middle of a blizzard. Heidi adopted her shortly thereafter. Annie loves to lie in the sunshine, groom Ernie Bert, show off her chipmunk cheeks, and pose for pictures. She was most likely a silent film actress or a mistress to a mobster in another life.

·   ·   ·

LIMERICK *(ALSO KNOWN as Limmy)* - Grandmummy's son, Heidi's and Auntie G's brother. Limerick is a Turkey Dog who was rescued in the same neighborhood as Ernie and by the same woman. After arriving in the United States in August 2018, he is now Ernie's mischievous sidekick. That said, we are fairly certain that he left a lengthy arrest record and several disgruntled girlfriends back in Turkey.

MR. BALLIE - ERNIE'S loyal companion and best friend. An orange and blue rubber ball from PetSmart that joined the family a few days after Ernie. It is impossible to put into words the bond between our protagonist and Mr. Ballie. Batman and Robin? Yoko and John? R2D2 and C3PO? No, it is not possible to describe nor equate. Just know that wherever Ernie is Mr. Ballie is nearby.

THEMES

Acceptance - Ernie Bert and Limerick learn to accept that they are far superior to their humans. They also learn to accept that their humans can be highly annoying, overly anxious, and incredibly stupid.

LOVE - READ THE BOOK. It's pretty obvious.

AMERICAN DREAM - From the streets of Istanbul to the townhouses of Virginia, this is a rags to lower-middle class story for the ages.

TERMS TO KNOW

Golden Retriever or Golden: a breed of dog that first appeared in Scotland. A dapper gentleman by the name of Lord Tweedmouth first bred the hunting dogs, and they quickly became a status symbol for the wealthy. We know them for their golden coats, muscular builds, and gentle natures. Many golden retrievers love the water and use their swimming skills to retrieve fowl for their owners. In our case, Ernie Bert despises the water and expects his owner to retrieve the fowl for him. Ernie is an anomaly, but, then again, everything with Ernie Bert is rare.

Turkey Dog: a dog from Turkey. Most of the time, these canines are left to fend for themselves until a kind soul rescues them. They roam in packs on the Turkish streets or in the forests and junkyards. Once the lucky few find shelter, several rescue organizations throughout the nation fly them to America. Sadly, the golden retriever is one of the breeds that is most often abandoned. As in America, they are viewed as status symbols, but it does not take long before their owners realize that the cute balls of fluff require a lot of hard work. Discouraged by this, many abandon their goldens, thus leaving thousands homeless and left to wander in search of safety. Due to their gentle nature, they cannot defend themselves like other breeds might and often perish from starvation, injury, abuse, or illness.

SYMBOLS

All great pieces of literature contain symbols. *The Scarlet Letter* has its "A." *The Great Gatsby* has its green light. *The*

Old Man and the Sea has its marlin. This book has nothing. Nada. Not one single remotely deep or semi-deep symbol. No hidden messages here. We are a completely surface-level, beach read, no-brain-cells-needed creation.

FREQUENTLY ASKED QUESTIONS

"A dog is not a thing. A thing is replaceable. A dog is not. A thing is disposable. A dog is not. A thing doesn't have a heart. A dog's heart is bigger than any 'thing' you can ever own."

~ Elizabeth Parker

How do I adopt a Turkey Dog?

As the plight of the Turkey Dogs becomes more well-known, more and more rescue organizations throughout the United States are seeking ways to help the four-legged orphans of Istanbul and her neighboring cities. The Southeastern Virginia Golden Retriever Rescue, Education & Training (SEVA GRREAT) organization in Yorktown, Virginia, is one that I have worked with extensively.

That said, there are numerous legitimate rescues throughout the nation that are rescuing dogs from Turkey and other locations, such as the China meat markets. You will want to do some research to make sure the rescue in your area follows all of the government protocols to bring the dog safely into the United States.

What is the adoption process like?

While the adoption process varies for each dog and situation, the basic steps are the same. The first thing you will need to do is determine whether you are willing and able to make a lifetime commitment to an animal. Adopting an animal is much like adopting a child. It is not a decision that anyone should take lightly. One should only proceed after giving it careful thought and consideration. Pet adoption can be wonderful. It can be life changing. It can offer some of the happiest moments of your life. However, it can also be frustrating and worrisome at times. After surveying your financial situation and heart and you find you are willing and able to dedicate your life to caring for a dog—especially a dog that may come with pre-existing health or social challenges—you will want to fill out the online application that most organizations have on their websites.

Once you have done this, it is important to remain patient during this time. Volunteers with full-time jobs run many of the Turkey Dog rescues, so the response time may be longer than if you were to adopt from a traditional shelter. Most work over forty hours per week in their full-time jobs and then dedicate the rest of their time to saving animals like Ernie Bert and Limerick.

If they approve your application, the rescue volunteers will conduct a home visit, interview, and reference checks. Depending on your location, a home visit may not be possible. In that case, most rescues will request photos or videos of your residence. They could also request a live video tour.

The last step, waiting, is the hardest. It is important that the rescue finds the perfect dog for you and your situation. For instance, I needed a dog that was good with cats. Others may need a senior dog who is calmer, while some may wish for a more energetic companion. The rescues also take into consideration the needs of the animal. If you remember from Ernie's story, I originally wanted to adopt a dog named Aslan. Since he was deaf, he found a home with an older dog who could guide him within his new surroundings. Therefore, it is important to remain open-minded and know that the right dog will find its way to you. Let the professionals and the universe find the perfect dog for you. In the end, you will be glad you did.

How should I prepare for my Turkey Dog's arrival?

Once you receive confirmation from your rescue, you will want to purchase a new bed, food and water bowls, leash, collar, name tag with important contact information, and several toys. You should also make an appointment with your vet within the first few days of your dog's arrival. While this medical visit may seem traumatic for an animal that has just traveled thousands of miles to a foreign country, it is vitally important that you put your new family member on a proper diet and schedule a thorough exam as soon as possible.

You should also plan to clear your calendar for at least three days to stay close to home. Turkey Dogs, like most shelter dogs, are usually timid of their new surroundings. However, unlike local shelter dogs, they also must acclimatize to a new country filled with unfamiliar smells, sounds, climates, languages, and food. Having you home with them for the welcome period will give you both an opportunity to bond and settle into a routine.

After my Turkey Dog's arrival, what should I expect?

The **rule of threes** is important to remember. The first **three days** are scary and exciting for your Turkey Dog. For quite some time, he had to fend for himself on the streets, and now he suddenly has fresh food and water, new areas to explore, and strange humans surrounding him. It is vital that you are patient and empathetic during this time.

That said, the first three days for Ernie were mostly joyful. At first, he was terrified to enter the house, but after some soft coaxing and praise, he soon found a new ball and began playing. On the second and third days, he spent most of the time sleeping. This is normal. The travel and new surroundings take a toll, so don't be surprised if your Turkey Dog sleeps for many hours during his first few days with you. This may be the first time in his life that he has had a warm bed, shelter, and a safe environment. He may also be suffering from jet lag, just like humans.

After **three weeks**, you and your Turkey Dog should be settling into a routine. You may notice that he has some bad habits that are typical of most dogs: chewing, marking territory, barking, etc. Continue to be patient, kind, and firm. Turkey Dogs are smart, but they like to test their humans.

I would not recommend starting an obedience class this soon in your journey together. Remember, your dog probably endured a great deal of trauma on the streets and is still trying to get used to a new culture. It is best to let him become comfortable with his surroundings before you add another variable to the mix.

After **three months**, your dog should feel comfortable and show you additional aspects of his personality. There will still be mishaps and challenges, but the love and gratitude he displays for you and your family are priceless. Quite simply, there is just something special about a Turkey Dog. It is as if he knows that the worst is behind him, and he knows he is one of the lucky ones to escape a life on the streets. Get ready to feel like the most important human being in the world—whether you deserve it or not.

What are Turkish commands for dogs?

When I adopted Ernie, I received a list of Turkish commands to use with him. In typical Ernie fashion, he ignored every one of them. However, your dog may be different. If so, you can try these out. Good luck!

Gel = come
Kal = stay
Otur = sit
Git = go
Seni seviyorum = I love you.

How can I help the Turkey Dog rescues?

Running a rescue is expensive and time-consuming. If you would like to help, making a monetary donation or volunteering your time are wonderful ways to help the Turkey Dogs and their champions.

If you travel to and from Turkey, you could also serve as a flight chaperone for a dog. This is an easy and cost-free way to help. Just let a Turkey Dog rescue know your flight details, and they will arrange to have a dog travel under your booking. This requires no cost or responsibility on your end. You simply agree to have a rescued dog travel under your name until he reaches his final destination.

Other ways to help may be to serve as a temporary foster, conduct a home visit, or transport the dogs to and from the airport. This gives you an opportunity to interact with the dogs and see wonderful adoptions in the making without the responsibility that comes with owning a dog.

Or, if you have your own Turkey Dog, you might write your own book. After all, every adoption story is priceless and deserves to be shared.

AUTHOR'S NOTE

Dear Reader,

I hope you enjoyed Ernie's story. Sadly, future stories like his will not be possible due to recent developments in the United States.

On June 14, 2021, the Centers for Disease Control and Prevention (CDC) issued a blanket decision to suspend the importation of dogs from 113 countries due to an alleged risk of rabies. This ban also affected US service men and women, diplomats, and government contractors who adopted dogs overseas and wanted to bring them home.

I understand it is the CDC's responsibility to keep all animals and Americans healthy and safe, and the reputable rescue organizations affected by this ban share the same goal. However, this ban is an overreach and is not supported by the CDC's actual rabies data. In the ban, the CDC itself admits that there is a "minuscule chance" of a dog arriving in America with rabies. Since 2016, there have only been four reported cases among the thousands upon thousands of dogs that have entered the country.

Dogs like Ernie Bert and Limerick who come from

legitimate agencies are compliant with government regulations. They are vaccinated for rabies and receive additional mandatory vaccinations and health screenings. They are regularly tested by veterinarians, have proper import permits, and are approved by the USDA before entering the country.

The international rescues need your help. They need the CDC to issue an exemption to the ban for the legitimate, non-profit rescue organizations who follow all the USDA guidelines and are committed to continuing to work with the CDC to ensure only healthy dogs are imported into the United States.

Leaving these dogs overseas is a death sentence. Please be an advocate in getting the CDC to issue an exemption for legitimate non-profit dog rescues by contacting your congressional representative or the CDC. Your help will impact the thousands of dogs relying on legitimate non-profits to give them a second chance.

Kind Regards,
Heidi

ACKNOWLEDGEMENTS

This little book is a labor of love, and it wouldn't have been possible without the support and guidance from so many wonderful individuals around the world.

Abundant thanks goes to my editor Helen Falconer. A year ago, I handed her a draft that was a jumbled mess of stories and confusing timelines. Through her guidance, I was able to restructure the book in a way that made sense. Her skill and encouragement during the writing process were invaluable, and I learned countless lessons under her tutelage. One day, I hope to enjoy a spot of tea with her in the lovely Irish countryside.

The cover design is the work of the talented Michael Rehder of Rehder and Companie in Canada. His vision far exceeded anything I could have imagined. I thoroughly enjoyed our collaboration, and I am so grateful for his artistic eye and attention to detail.

This book offered me the opportunity to revisit my early teaching days with two of my favorites. Many thanks goes to my proofreader (and former colleague!) Melinda Shenkkan and her former student, Leigh Ann Burdett, who took the photo on the back cover.

Dr. Brittany Ashworth, Dr. Matt Williams, and the amazing staff at Poquoson Veterinary Hospital continue to offer Ernie and his siblings the best medical care possible, and I am incredibly grateful for the kindness they show to me and my furry family.

To everyone who has followed Ernie's adventures on Facebook, thank you for being animal lovers and lifting us up when we were down, laughing at our shenanigans, and loving Ernie Bert along with me.

To the international rescues and volunteers — especially Michelle and Chari — I hope you realize the countless lives you are impacting with your selfless work. Your tireless efforts are saving not only dogs but humans, as well.

Fairy Godmother, none of this would have been possible without your enormous heart, hopeful vision, boundless energy, and unwavering determination. You are Wonder Woman, an angel, and the Fairy Godmother wrapped into one. Thank you for rescuing Ernie, Limerick, and the hundreds of other doggies. You are remarkable.

Although they are no longer with us, I like to think that my grandparents were watching over me when I adopted Ernie and wrote our story. My fondest childhood memories were spent at their home in Virginia, and I never will be able to put into words what they meant to me. I definitely won the grandparent lottery with Muckie and Bobby.

To my sister, Gretchen, thanks for putting up with my Barbie stealing, arm biting, hair pulling, and name calling for so many years. I know you always have my back, and I will always have yours.

Before Ernie Bert, there was Buddy, Huey, Charlie,

Annie, Termite, and many others. Their unconditional love gave me so much joy and comfort. I know one day I will see them at the Rainbow Bridge. Until then, I will continue to try to live by the lessons they taught me.

Finally, I never would have written a page of this book if it hadn't been for my mother. She has always encouraged my writing and believed in me when I didn't. Mom, I am so lucky to have you as my mother, role model, and best friend. One day, I hope to be half the woman that you are.

And, Ernie Bert...we did it, big guy. Let's go play fetch.

ENJOY THIS BOOK?
YOU CAN MAKE A BIG DIFFERENCE!

Honest reviews of our book, help bring it to the attention of other readers. It is one of the most powerful tools I have to spread the word of these amazing rescues.

If you enjoyed *My Journey with Ernie*, I would be incredibly grateful if you would take five minutes to leave a review on Amazon. It can be as long or as short as you wish!

Thank you very much!

GET TWO DELETED EXCERPTS AND
AN EXCLUSIVE NEWSLETTER!

Building a relationship with fellow animal lovers is one of the best things about writing this book. I will occasionally send out newsletters with Ernie Bert updates, Limerick shenanigans, Grandmummy-isms, travel accounts, and other fun tidbits.

And if you sign up to our mailing list, I'll send you two deleted excerpts for free.

You can get this by visiting www.heidihspeece.com and signing up!

ABOUT THE AUTHOR

Raised in rural Nebraska, **Heidi H. Speece** received her Masters degree from the University of Pittsburgh and is currently a high school English teacher. When not playing fetch with Ernie, she enjoys traveling and photography. She lives in Virginia with Ernie Bert and her two cats, Lottie and Louis. This is Heidi's debut book, and a majority of the proceeds will be donated to animal rescues.

 facebook.com/heidihspeece
instagram.com/heidihspeece